ABOUT THE AUTHOR

The author was born in [...] troubled childhood and [...] home at 15 with no educat[ion...] knowledge of the outside world.
She was married at 19 and now has three grown up children.
In recent years, mainly due to an accident at work which has left her in constant pain, she has found great pleasure in writing. Most of her writing to date has been religious, for her own spiritual growth, and to help others in need of spiritual guidance.
"A Saint I Ain't" is her autobiography, written partly because of her brother's tragic death in 1995, and partly to fulfil a need for her family to know just why their love is so important to her.

A SAINT I AIN'T

A Saint I Ain't

by

Mary G MacKiever

Central Publishing Limited
West Yorkshire

© Copyright 2001
Mary G MacKiever

The right of Mary G MacKiever to be identified as
author of this work has been asserted by her in accordance with
Copyright, Designs and Patents Act 1988

All rights reserved. No reproduction,
copy or transmission of this publication may be made
without written permission. No paragraph of this publication may be
reproduced, copied or transmitted
save with the written permission or in accordance
with the provisions of the Copyright Act 1956 (as amended). Any person
who does any unauthorised act
in relation to this publication may be liable
to criminal prosecution and civil
claims for damage.

First published by Hamilton & Co. Publishers Ltd
ISBN 1 901668 53 3

Second Edition
Paperback ISBN 1 903970 35 0

*Published
by*

Central Publishing Limited
Royd Street Offices
Milnsbridge
Huddersfield
West Yorkshire
HD3 4QY

www.centralpublishing.co.uk

A Saint I Ain't

Chapter 1

I have on my fridge one of those quotes which help you through the slog of daily life. I have no idea who wrote it, but its sentiment appeals to me. It is entitled "One day at a time". Briefly it says there are two days in the week about which we should not worry. Yesterday and Tomorrow. Yesterday, with all its cares and mistakes has passed forever. We cannot erase a single word. Yesterday has gone. Tomorrow is beyond our immediate control. It will come, but is as yet unborn. This leaves only one day, today. Let us therefore live for today. This seems a very simple, but profound statement; easy to say, but not so easy to put into practice. It is the most natural thing for every human being to be sorry that they said or did something wrong yesterday, meaning to put it right tomorrow. But as we all know too well, tomorrow always brings its own problems. It's not what you do today that will lead you to despair, it's the remorse and bitterness for something which happened yesterday, and the dread of what tomorrow might bring, which will be your downfall. It is when we allow the burdens of these two days to get us down that we are on the way to a breakdown.

There have been times in recent years when I have allowed the memories of my past and the fears of my future to bring so much dread into the thought of tomorrow that I have been unable to cope with daily living. Thankfully those times are behind me at the moment and I am getting on with what is to be the rest of my future. The pattern of my early childhood and throughout my teens to my becoming a young woman, has been, to say the least, unusually traumatic.

Mary MacKiever

I was born in Scotland in 1953. I was named Mary after my father's sister whom I grew to know and love more than any other of my relatives.

1953 was the year Edmund Hillary conquered Mt Everest and of course the year that the Princess who drove trucks in the war rode to her Coronation in a golden coach pulled by eight grey horses, to be crowned Queen Elizabeth II on June 2nd at Westminster Abbey. It was watched by millions of people all over the world.

My parents and my two older brothers, Robert, who was four and David who was a year and a day younger, aged three, might have watched it. I like to think they did. I, however, was not destined to be a princess, I was never to marry a prince. I rather suspect that my mother and father wouldn't have owned a television set in those days. I believe only the very rich could have afforded one. My family were not rich.

My father was a soldier in the Second World War. I never knew what he did for a living before the war or how he served as a soldier, not even the regiment he was in, but I believe he was abroad in India at some time. He was one of a large family. He has at least three sisters, and I'm not sure how many brothers, but there were a lot. I cannot remember ever meeting my grandfather, but I do remember vividly the only time I met my grandmother. I must have been very young, no more than three or four years old. I was made to sit on her knee. I was very frightened of her because she was very old and looked like a skeleton and I cried and tried to pull away from her. Thinking back now, this might have been the first time she had seen me. The whole episode was one of a strained uncomfortable meeting for everybody. The house was dark and tiny. She seemed to be tiny too. She was wearing a dark coloured thick dress with a grey or cream-coloured pinny which crossed at the back. She had a scarf over her head and her face was thin and wrinkled with a sharp jaw and sunken eyes. I remember thinking she would hurt me and I don't believe I ever saw her again.

My mother spoke little of her family. I never met any of them.

A Saint I Ain't

They didn't approve of her friendship with my father. She told me that her parents were strict church attenders and they disapproved of my father because even when she first met him, my father was a heavy drinker. Even her brothers and sisters, to whom she had been very close, would not be able to see her again if she continued to see him. She had been told by the church minister that she could not have communion if she disobeyed her parents. I also know that they lived together before they were married because my eldest brother Robert found out while looking through my mother's divorce papers that the date of their wedding was after he was born.

Robert and David were born in Yorkshire. My father had come down, like hundreds of Scots in the late '40s and early '50s, to find work in the Yorkshire coal mines. I don't know if he was already a miner, or if he came just to find work and a house, or if this was the place some of his friends had come to already. He stayed in contact with his family who lived in Fife, just outside Edinburgh. My mother was never to see any of her family, who were from Aberdeen, again.

I was born in Scone in the county of Perth, on Friday 13th March 1953. Why they were back in Scotland, I have no idea, but by some strange turn of fate I was the only one of the six of us to be born on Scottish soil, the three that were to follow were all born in Yorkshire, where we moved to when I was just a baby.

I remember little about my first five years, except the visit to my grandmother. I do however recall a shopping trip when I was bought a green coat with a black or dark brown velvet collar and a fur muff (hand warmer) to match. I told my mother that I remember shopping for this coat and she said I could have been no more than three and my Auntie Mary had bought it for me when she came to stay with us for a holiday. Auntie Mary came to stay again when I was much older. When she stayed we had treats like cakes, biscuits, lemonade and crisps. I even remember during one such holiday, a trip to a local park and a ride on the donkeys. I learned to my dismay much later that Auntie Mary had wanted me to live with her and Uncle Bob, but my parents refused. It seems ironic to me that she and Uncle Bob were unable to have children and would have made perfect parents, and that her brother fathered six and didn't give a damn about any of them. Just goes to show, life isn't fair.

I was not quite five when I began school. I was pushed in the door by my mother and left. My teacher was very kind and gentle to me. I remember her now. On my fifth birthday my teacher gave me a bag with an apple and an orange in it.

I was good at reading and writing but I couldn't count, I still can't. I can smell the aroma of the varnished desk, and the smell of the wax crayons and the books come to my senses as if it were yesterday. I remember the Janet and John books we learned to read from and the play times when we were allowed to ride bikes and play with thick wooden hoops. One of our dinner ladies who played with us had the middle fingers of her hand missing and when we joined hands to play Lucy Locket lost her pocket, it felt funny. She only had a little finger and a thumb on one hand. Funny the things you remember, isn't it?

By the time I was seven, I had two more brothers and a sister. They were Paul, Jill and Philip.

I don't remember my mother being pregnant with any of my siblings, but on the day Philip was born all the rest of the children were sent out of the house all day. Paul, Robert, David and me stayed in the garden all day long. We weren't told why of course, we didn't ask. Children weren't told about babies in those days. We just went out to play. We made a boat out of an old tin bath I remember. We all sat in it and rocked it. We pretended we were on the sea, we were pirates of course. The day must have flown. It was late in the afternoon when we were called in and shown this baby. Philip was a fat baby with curly fair hair. That night he cried all night and we thought he sounded like a duck quacking.

On the day Philip was born Jill must have gone to a neighbours to be looked after. She was still a baby. Mum told us many years later about the day Jill was born. The doctor had to be sent for because she was too small. I don't know if this was because she was premature or because my mother did not take care or herself while she was pregnant. Jill was taken to the village clinic when she was a few days old. She weighed just two and a half pounds and my mother was told to take her straight home as she was not expected to live. All babies have a soft spot just above the forehead which has a thin layer of skin over it. This is called the fontanel. This closes during the first few months of life. Somehow Jill's was too large and didn't close as it should. She was always a sickly child, but she did live. The only thing I think of when I think of her as a baby was that she cried all day and all night. She was born in the night because I remember being woken by a very excited Robert and David who thought we had got a new puppy which they had been asking for. In the cold light of day, we found out it was not a cuddly puppy they heard, it was a squealing baby which was going to go on squealing for years. Maybe that's why we never really warmed to her, we would rather have had a puppy. As she grew into a toddler, she used to have temper tantrums and we would say, " Jill's having a paddy again." Even when she started school, the teachers used to send for me or Paul to take her home because she wouldn't stop crying.

Even in those early years I remember the arguments and physical fights my parents had. We lived in a three-bedroomed house on a typical pit housing estate. My father spent much of his time working down the pit. When he wasn't working he was in the bookies or the pub. The betting hut was conveniently situated at the bottom of our garden. The fence had been broken down by the constant stream of people that used our garden as a path to the bookies or the beer-off next to it. Eventually he got barred from all the pubs in the surrounding area and had to go into town to the pub.

Summer was an exciting time for the children of the village. Almost as soon as school broke up for the six weeks holidays, preparations would begin for the annual Pit Gala. Even in a household like ours where happy days were few and far between, the Gala was something we all had a part to play in. Each year there would be a float; open lorries, one from each street, decorated with different themes each year, which were driven slowly in a huge convoy through the village to the fields near the colliery where almost all the men in the village worked. There we would have races and games all day on Gala day. Prizes, awards and cups were won. All the children, babies and toddlers through to teenagers were given presents and various sweets. There was the pit band playing all day and other live music and dancing. I remember clearly a man talking through a megaphone, announcing winners, results of competitions and lost children, the fancy dress winners and the most important was the prize for the best float. One year when I was about seven, I was chosen to be on the float. That year the theme was the Arabian Knights. I was a dancing girl and Robert, David and Paul were knights. Jill and Philip were too young. Because all the street was involved in the Gala and in those days the average miners family had little money to spare, everyone helped to raise money towards prizes and costumes for the float. There was street bingo held in people's houses. This was the only time I remember us mixing with the neighbours – well, going into their houses anyway. We had bring and buys and street jumble sales. All money raised went towards decorating the lorry and making the outfits for us to wear. My costume was a mauve coloured top and baggy trousers in a kind of silk material, covered with netting. My hair was permed using a foul smelling lotion and pipe cleaners. It was a long, smelly, painful process which haunts me to this day still. I wore pink plastic shoes and a silk scarf over my head held down by a tiara, and a piece of netting across my mouth. Sounds awful but I looked and felt like an Arabian dancing girl. I stood in my place on the lorry and was paraded through the streets with pride. That particular Gala Day remains one of the best days I remember.

As a child, I was not aware that the neighbours were talking about us, but I know now that they were. I met a lady quite recently who remembered our family. They felt sorry for my mum, she said, who had to live with a drunken bully of a husband. The fights were loud and often in the night when sound carries more. The next day he would go off to work and mum, regularly nursing a black eye or other such injuries, would carry on her daily life as if it were quite normal. Sometimes if he wasn't

A Saint I Ain't

at work they would fight during the day. We were used to seeing mum throw the odd milk bottle or two, often hitting the target, dad's head, blood dripping on the stone kitchen floor. Dad retaliating with a similar heavy object, at the same time hurling obscene verbal abuse at one another. It was all part of their daily routine. We usually just kept out of the way until it stopped.

One summer when I was about eight years old, we had a break from home life and went on our one and only holiday. Dad had paid the deposit on a caravan owned by a lady up the street. It was to be a week in Cleethorpes. But the rest of the money for the van never came and mum had to tell the lady we couldn't go. The lady felt sorry for her and let us go free of charge. So mum scraped together the train fare and the holiday was on. Dad came with us in the train, but I'll never know why. He came home the next day leaving his wife and six children with no money or food, just the return tickets home. I wonder now if the woman who owned the van gave mum some money and he took it and went home. It left us stranded in Cleethorpes penniless and starving. After the second day, me and the boys went onto the beach and picked cockles and took them back for mum to boil. We all ate them. Unfortunately they gave every one of us, including mum, diarrhoea and sickness. Somehow the family in the caravan next door found out and they sent us food. We had a Kellogg's variety pack, a treat we never had at home, tinned meats, fruit and cheese. We ate better than we did at home all week. Mum reminded him and us forever that she took the name and address of these kind people so as to repay the money, but he tore it up so she never could. That will be a holiday I will never forget.

I do remember another train journey, though some years before the ill-fated holiday. It too was a trip to Cleethorpes, when I was about three years old. Our father was a member of the local working men's club and each year they had a day trip to the seaside. All the families in the village were going. We got on the train at the station. It was a green steam train I remember. I can't recall many of the events of the day except the train station and an incident on the beach much later in the day. I remember clearly seeing a little boy falling down some concrete steps on the beach. His head was bleeding and as I watched, his mother picked him up and took him away. Later on when we were trying to find an empty compartment on the train for the journey home, we ended up sharing a compartment with the little boy who had fallen down, and his mother and brother. My mum asked the lady if the little boy was all right. Unknown to any of us, this was the little boy I was to marry many years later. Both of us remember the mums talking, as our mothers did when we recalled this.

Can we really say we were destined to marry?

Times were hard for a lot of families in the late fifties, but looking back now, it wasn't just hard times we were having. Our parents were seriously neglecting us even then in ways both physical and emotional. For one thing, we were starved.

We were used to going without food at home. We would go outside and eat anything we could find. Me and the boys (Robert and David were always referred to as "the boys" when we were at home) would steal from the local farmers' fields, eating raw cabbage or turnips. In summer we raided the apple and pear trees from the gardens around the village. Even the well fed kids nicked the apples and pears, it was a great game to us all. The local bobby who lived near us "clipped" mine and the boys ear more than once, along with the other kids he managed to catch as we ran away, not quite fast enough. Sometimes our father would take us up on the coal tip to pick coal which we would burn or sell. I knew the difference between coal and what he called shale which was stone that looked like coal but was heavier and if it went on the fire, it would spark and crack and jump out of the grate into the room. Although we were given free loads of coal as all miners were, our father would sell it by the barrow full at ten bob a barrow so he could have his drink or bookie money. Coal was the only form of heating in the house, and it heated the water. We mainly used the fire to boil the kettle tea (which only they had) and we kids drank water.

Just our immediate neighbours seemed to know about his temper. He always had a laugh and a joke with everyone as he walked down the street. The people called him Mr Mac. My mother was known as Mrs Mac to our neighbours. She brainwashed us into calling him "the old pig", a term we used if we ever had to refer to him, until she died. I don't remember her calling him anything else while they were together or after the family split up. To his face she called him Mac, but to us she used to say, "if you don't behave, I'll tell the old pig," or, "go and get the old pig up for work, Mary." Our parents were so wrapped up in their hatred of each other that they forgot or simply didn't care about us. Nobody cared about us. Looking back now, it's a wonder any of us survived, not just Jill.

They were very strict about us keeping our Scottish accent. We were living in a Yorkshire pit village populated mainly with Yorkshire people. Our teachers, shopkeepers, doctors and most of our friends spoke with the local dialect, but we were discouraged by our parents. As we grew older we learned to speak Yorkshire outside the house and Scottish inside. If we were out with our parents, we had to speak Scottish in front of our friends. This could be embarrassing but we got used to it. We kept many of the traditions which characterised a typical Scottish family.

It is said the Scots are mean with money. Well, I remember one occasion when they literally threw money away. When a bride leaves the house on her way to her wedding, friends and neighbours, and their children, line the pavement and pennies are thrown. These are gathered up after the car, or more usually in our street the horse and cart, has gone past. This is meant to symbolise wealth for the happy couple I believe.

Horse and carts were used commonly as transport then, much as lorries are now. Our family moved when I was young, from one side of the village to the other. We went from the more posh side, where a large proportion of the estate were Scottish people, to the side which was much rougher and was a more Yorkshire dominated area. I am not sure why we moved, but I suspect we were unable to pay the higher rent on the more posh side. We were moved by a funny little man with a horse and cart. When moving day came, all our belongings were piled onto the cart, then all the six children and our parents climbed on and we were taken to our second home. We children thought it was fun, but I feel it was not the same for our parents who, I feel sure, didn't want to go. Although times were not easy in the '50s, I saw that most of our neighbours seemed better off than us for some reason. Our next door neighbours had their elderly parents living with them. The old lady, who we called Granny, died. Our mother didn't go to the house before or after the funeral. She was very superstitious about death. Here, incidentally, was another use of the horse and cart. The horse had a large brass harness and a big black plume on its head and it transported the coffin to church. There was a gathering in Granny's house afterwards. When everyone had gone home, we were sent trays of unwanted food. My mother threw it away all because it was from Granny's death.

The rag man was another man who used a horse and cart to ply his trade. He came around the streets of the village collecting old clothes and other unwanted small household items that people wanted to get rid of. We called him the balloon man as he gave balloons on sticks to the children who took out the rags.

School life in general was bad for a family like ours. Corporal punishment was the norm then. There were two or three of us in my class who seemed to get more of it than others, I never did know why. Public beatings and humiliation were meted out to the likes of us so often that it seemed natural.

"Where's your trip money Mary?" they would ask. I knew better than to ask for money at home so I would say, "I've forgotten it."

"Where's your PE kit Mary?"

"I've forgotten it."

I spent most games lessons and sports days picking up litter from the school yard for not having shorts. When the others went on school trips, I sat at the back of someone else's class for 'forgetting' my trip money. We weren't the only family like that, they were quite common at that time. But there was something different about our family, I sensed it. Even in the infants school, I wanted to run away. Our clothes were dirty. We were never encouraged to wash. I had only one set of underclothes that were washed once a week, on Sunday, ready for school on Monday. The teachers picked on us. I was told off so often sometimes for something little and once I had my knuckles rapped with a wooden ruler for not being able to do my sums. One memorable day, me and another girl were caught by a teacher doing what we all did, running all the taps at once in the girls toilets. We were both dragged literally by the ears in front of the class. We were both smacked painfully on the tops of our bare legs, for all to see, then made to stand in a corner all lesson. Well, at least we had done something that time! I once got slippered for answering back a teacher. Me and the boys would meet up in the playground and tell what kind of a day we were having. It wasn't only me and the boys this happened to, many other children were treated this way, it was all part of growing up.

Things got progressively worse at home as we got older. Perhaps they just seemed worse or maybe my parents' marriage was getting unbearable, I don't know. His drinking was getting worse and was definitely causing real problems. They had loud verbal and physical fights about this. Our needs as growing children were not being met and my mother knew this. It must have had an effect on her. She couldn't give us what we needed, so she argued with him and took it out on us!

We never had anything to eat before going to school that's for sure. We didn't get free dinners like some children did because our father had a good job at the pit. He had to keep working to bring in the drinking money. The agony of smelling the wonderful aroma of school dinners, starving hungry, being told by our mother not to bother coming home at dinner time because there wouldn't be any food till supper time. Then it might be boiled sausages and boiled potatoes if we were lucky. A plate of baked beans was a regular meal, with a slice of dry bread. Bread was always rationed in our house. The slices were counted so we daren't pinch it. We never had fresh fruit or veg of any kind. Milk we got at school free, as you did in school in the fifties. At home we never had breakfast or a Sunday dinner. Some food our mother would hide "so that the old pig didn't get it." I'm sure there were times when she did try to look after us, but these times seemed few and far between. I know times were hard in those days, especially with six children to feed, but even considering all the circumstances, we were not cared for as we should have been.

Every day was the same. It was out of bed, get dressed, downstairs, straight out the front door, no wash or anything, then run all the way to school. My brothers used to hit me on the way to school because they had to take me, and every day we were late. I slowed them up even more. They knew that they, like me, would be in trouble as soon as we reached the classroom, so they took it out on me. Angry and frustrated we ran to school day after day, winter and summer alike. Pushed and pulled along by my brothers all the way to school. Running through the empty playground, then we would go our separate ways into our classrooms, me and the boys.

"Late again Mary," the teacher said each day, "stand in the corner."

I knew that corner so well.

"Why don't you set your alarm clock earlier?" she would say! That's a laugh, I thought, silently facing the wall. Alarm clock, in our house? Some nights I didn't get to sleep till after ten or even midnight. Dad came in from the pub. The nightly row began. Short or long, physical or verbal, either way we listened, all huddled in one bedroom. Swearing and abuse hurled at one another, dad beat mum, mum beat dad, then they went to bed, or not as the case may be.

In my bed there was Jill on one side of me and Philip on the other. No pampers in those days. Wet nappies or wet knickers from them. It was hard luck for me. No wonder I smelt. I never wet the bed, but I slept in one! Winter time was bad. It was cold and damp. Night times were hell, old coats for blankets, no sheets on the bed, no pillows, just old rags stuffed into dirty pillowcases. Summer wasn't much better. It was as bad to be hot in a damp bed as cold. I would lie in bed at night and think, I'll run away one day.

A Saint I Ain't

Junior school was worse. Children can be very cruel. Me and Robert and David stayed in the playground together. By now we wanted people to know how bad things were at home. We spent every hour we could out of the house. Our father had started to beat the boys (the boys being Robert and David, not Paul or Philip). He would take off his big leather pit belt and let fly at them for almost anything. I used to watch him leather them and I would cry and cover my ears when they screamed out in pain for him to stop. He never hit me, my mother did that and boy, could she hit where it hurt. We hated them now. As far as I remember they never hit the little ones, just us three, then they would hit each other. What a sad life we had.

When the boys went up to the secondary school I was devastated. I really was alone now. No one to run to school with, Paul went on his own and our mother took Jill. Philip was still too young to go to school. So I went on my own every day. There was no one at play time to share the morning's events. I had to bear the hunger pangs throughout the dinner break alone. Also we had to get used to the cruel bullying and name calling from the other children. The boys would bash some of the culprits, but I couldn't. I ran away and hid every day, alone. No one liked me and I didn't blame them. They used to call us the "Mucky Macs".

Not all the memories of my younger days are of bad things though. When I was about eight, Paul and I were out walking one hot sunny summer evening. We came across a group of children who were around our age, sitting on a grassy bank singing songs. A man was playing a guitar and they all looked very happy. Paul and I sat at the back listening. We didn't know any of the children, they weren't from our school. No sooner had we sat down when the singing stopped and the man with the guitar said, "That's all kids, it's time to go home. See you all on Tuesday."

I asked the girl sitting in front of me what was happening on Tuesday.

"It's the Tuesday Club, " she replied. This, she told me was a children's club run at the local Methodist Church in the village next to ours. I decided there and then that I was going. I liked what I saw of these people straight away. Remember that we're talking about the late fifties. Kids as young as seven or eight like me and Paul went all over on our own then. Times have changed now. So many bad things happen now, and probably did then, that parents keep a closer eye on where their children are, and who they are with. Now there are so many rules and regulations set in place to protect children, and rightly so, that clubs such as this one would have to meet certain criteria to open. A ratio of adults to children, males to females, health and safety, first aid training for leaders, hygiene certificates, all to protect leaders and children. Sometimes these rules and regulations act to reinforce fear and prejudice, but this was not so when the Tuesday Club was running. Never in all the years I went, did anything wrong or improper take place. My involvement with the club and its leaders was going to be one of the major influences on me, and would change my life forever. There I found true love and affection. I also found faith. Theirs and mine. These people loved me as I was; sad and dirty, an innocent child. They showed me God's love too. Here I began to believe in God.

On Tuesday I just turned up with the twenty or so other children. Paul didn't go. The man with the guitar was there, I found out he was "Uncle Tom ". There was also "Uncle Len" and their wives Elaine and Irene and their children, who were about my age or a bit older. They led a happy band of children both at this Tuesday Club and on a Sunday as well.

The Tuesday Club was well organised and well run. I liked Uncle Tom best. He was always laughing. I wished he was my dad. The four of them as a team taught us stories and songs about Jesus and other stories and people in the bible. They used felt cut-outs of people and animals and used pictures and drawings to show us the things the bible said. If we answered questions correctly, read well or wrote or drew something really well, we were given tokens. We collected these tokens and exchanged them for small badges, rubbers and pencils, book marks and prayer cards. Even small books sometimes. These little things I treasured. At home we had few toys and books of our own. We shared a few bits such as a Meccano set we got from somewhere and dinky cars we fought over. In fact my sister Jill used to wrap a milk bottle up in old rags and pretend it was a doll. We never celebrated our birthdays until much later on in life. We knew when they were, but they came and went like any other day. Also we were told that Scots folk don't celebrate Christmas, they see the New Year in instead. No Christmas dinner was ever cooked in our house; no Christmas pudding or tree or trimmings, nothing. We knew everyone else did but we never told anyone that we didn't have these things. We did have all the usual celebrations at school and now at church, but not at home. I got presents from my friends at church but I hid them so the others didn't find out and would take or break them.

Chapter 2

I was now reaching an age when I was feeling embarrassed and angry at my home situation. I never spoke about it to anyone. I wanted to tell Uncle Tom and the others, but I never quite knew what to say. They must have known much of the problems we were having as a family. Sometimes they gave me bags of clothes which their children, and others, had outgrown. Our mother accepted them happily, but soon they looked and smelt just like our old clothes. Our father saw the church folk as a way of getting money for drink. I know mum didn't like him doing it, but he would make me to go their homes with little notes which said, "Please can you let us have a couple of pounds to buy food for the children?" or, "Will you buy a barrow of coal?"

Sometimes they did, sometimes they gave me bread or food to take home with me or simply wrote back, "Sorry, we can't." They weren't stupid. They knew what he wanted it for. I hated taking these notes, but I had to. I think they did give my mother money sometimes but even so, she hated me going to the church. She tried to stop me but I went anyway. She never knew where we were when we were out anyway. I think she was angry because she had lost not only her family when she married my father, but her faith too. When I was older, she told me that she blamed God for everything. So here I was finding a faith of my own and she was still being deprived of the sacraments of the church because she had been living in sin. Even now that she was married, her family and the church, both which meant so much to her, had disowned her. Perhaps in her twisted and bitter mind, she thought keeping me from God would pay them back, I don't know. Well God will have the last word I can assure you.

I will never understand my mother. Her life must have been a daily hell. She had six children to a man she hated. She must have loved him at one time, but now that love had gone forever. She had given up her own family for love of him. Did she really believe she could change him, stop him drinking and make him be a good husband and father? Things were now so bad that she had eventually turned bitter. I remember seeing her spitting in his food while she was preparing a meal for him. The boys and I laughed. We hated him too, maybe because our mother did, but I for one had other reasons to hate him. Sometimes the boys and me would get revenge on him when he was too drunk to realise what we were doing. We would start some pretend game off with him asking what he did in the war, then all three of us would get him down on the floor and kick, bite and scratch him, pull his hair and not get off till he was really mad. Then we ran away. We knew we would get it if he caught us but he never did, we could run fast and in his drunken stupor we had an advantage and used the opportunity when we could. We would wait until he went out to the pub, then sneak upstairs until it was safe to come down. We never really knew how our mother would be, just because she was unhappy there was no need to make our lives a living hell as well.

One morning she called us and said, "You'd better keep out of the old pig's way today." It transpired that the evening before he had been scrounging money off some young lads in the pub and they said they would give him a couple of quid if he would let them cut his hair. As he was well drunk already, he said yes. They had shaved all his hair off. Now, the morning after, he was going to kill them and we would do best to keep out of his sight when he was in one of these moods. He had a thick mop of ginger hair, well he did have until that morning. We heard him cursing and swearing and our mother screeching that it served him right. They would row all day and probably the next as well. We were intrigued to see what he looked like but he wouldn't come out of the bedroom. When he eventually emerged the boys thought it was funny, but they kept their distance, not daring to let him see them laugh. We knew how far to go and this time we kept well back. When I saw him for the first time I was really frightened of him. He looked awful, totally bald, and very mad. I didn't laugh. I was only six or seven at the time and I scared easily. He refused to go out, not even to work. He got a Trilby - a man's hat with a wide brim - and he wore this everywhere to cover his badly cut hair, he even wore it if someone came to the house, he was so embarrassed about his hair loss.

One day me and the boys hid this hat and he was smashing the house up and accusing mum of moving it. He needed to go for some booze and he couldn't without the hat. We would have to give it back to him. Then Robert came up with an idea. While they were occupied shouting at each other, Robert threw the hat up on top of the lamp-post right outside our front window. It was an hour or more before he saw it. He wouldn't go out into the street even to retrieve it, in case the neighbours saw him bald. Mum refused to get it and eventually he rushed out and back in two seconds. We were crouching under the neighbour's garden wall, listening to him roaring with anger, threatening death to the one who had done it, blaming mum, saying that she wanted to humiliate him, and she screaming abuse back at him. Soon the hat was on and he stormed off to the pub All three of us were in hysterics. We would suffer for this, but at that moment we were revelling in our achievement. We all got a thrashing from mum, who never did find out which one of us it was!

Me and the boys seemed to get more than our fair share of beatings. We did get up to some mischief I admit, but for the most part we didn't deserve what we got. Sometimes when we knew we were going to get belted we would cover up for each other. I would go up to the bedroom to one of my favourite hiding places, which was under the mattress on one of the double beds. I remember the many times I have laid between the springs and the mattress. Mum or dad would come looking for me and I would lie there so still, hardly breathing, until they had gone. They would come up to the bed, even look under the bed, but they never found me, silent, between the spring base and the mattress. Sometimes one or both of the boys would actually sit on the bed with me under them saying, "We've not seen her."

I covered for them too. We hid in the sideboard in the front room, surrounded by the clothes kept in there. This was a good place to stay, and there was room for two. Then when all was clear we would sneak out of the house and off down the lanes for the rest of the day. Dad was usually too drunk to remember why he was looking for us, but mum, she never forgot. Up to a day or two after some misdemeanour had taken place, usually when I wasn't expecting it, she would drag me into the bedroom saying, "You thought I'd forgotten so and so you did yesterday, well I haven't," and I would get a good hiding, which I didn't know was coming.

She must have taken much of her anger at our father out on me and the boys. The boys got it worse though. They got belted by the old pig, I didn't. We all cried for each other, and so very often I wished I was dead.

From a very young age I was friendly with a boy called Andrew. He didn't go to our school, his family were Catholic and he went to the Catholic school in the next village. Andrew and I were the same age, in fact I was eight days older than him. He had an older brother who was married, so there was only him left at home. He was treated as an only child. His parents were always nice to me. His father was very quiet, as Andrew was, and unlike most of the men, he worked in town, in an office I think. His mum was a bright and cheerful lady and to me they seemed very well off. Andrew got everything he wanted and he had spending money, which he used to buy records. We spent many evenings together as we got older and, during the school holidays when his parents were out, he and I would sit in his front room and play records. Deep down I was jealous of the attention and love he got from his parents. I felt sort of privileged or honoured that he wanted me as his special friend. He would never know this. At weekends and holidays we played together. We listened to his radio in the street and sang and danced to the pop music, we would mime to the records of the day. This was the era when Matt Munro and The Beverley Sisters were being replaced with The Rolling Stones and their rivals The Beatles. Dancing the night away at the palais in slacks and petticoats had been replaced by Rock 'n' Roll, it was a very exciting time for kids our age. Mods and Rockers were fighting in the cities and seaside towns. But for Andrew and me, all our spare time was taken up with listening to or talking about pop music. I was really happy when I was with him. Together, at his expense, we went to see the Beatles films; Hard Days Night and Help. We also went to see Mary Poppins and the Sound of Music, but I won't talk about that.

One day during the summer when we were about ten years old, Andrew and I went for a walk to the nearby woods where we loved to play. It was a favourite place for all the kids. We often went there together. We climbed trees, played great hiding games, made dens and tree houses and would stay there all day long sometimes. These were innocent times for Andrew and me. We were just like brother and sister. In the woods this particular day, we climbed to the top of a high tree. From there we could see what we thought was a nearby castle. As it turned out it was the tower of a church just three quarters of a mile away. Nevertheless, we decided that it was this castle and we would go and visit it. It was also the era of Robin Hood, William Tell and Ivanhoe on the television. Knights and maidens were often included in our games and fantasies. We wanted to see a real castle.

It must have been late afternoon when we set out on our very own adventure, and we had no idea of the trouble we would get into. When we reached the church we realised the mistake we had made. We thought that the castle couldn't be that far away so we decided to carry on and go there anyway. As it turned out it was many miles away. We saw the signs for it and, driven on by the thrill and excitement of the adventure, we went on, and on, and on, until at last we arrived at the castle, only to find it had closed at five o'clock. Even if it had been open, it was sixpence to get in. Neither of us had a penny on us, or a watch for that matter. By now it must have been after six.

The long walk home began with a song and a laugh. After about four miles or so we began to feel hungry and tired. No food, no money, we carried on, not really knowing where we were or the way home. It must have been nine o'clock when we reached the church which we had mistaken for the castle. It was mid-summer so it was still light. We carried on for another mile or so until we reached the next village. We were too frightened to go back to the woods as it was now getting dark. We decided to walk up the lanes between this village and the village where we lived. These were at least a mile or two of dark, unlit lanes. Now we were really hungry and tired and frightened too. With about a mile to go we began to see strange threatening shadows in the bushes and fields. It was now much after ten and it was very dark. Walking up the pitch-black lanes with fields and woods all around us, we hid in the hedges if a car came past. We began to think we might get murdered or something. We then, and only then, thought we might be in trouble as we realised that we would now have been missed by our parents. So on we went shivering with cold and with fear. Our parents had of course missed us. We had been gone since early morning. It was unusual for us to be out all day long, and this was the first time we had been out after dark. We had usually been driven home to Andrew's long before supper time, our empty tummies being our alarm clock. The police had been notified and everyone was our looking for us. But not down the lanes where we were. We had started off in the opposite direction and gone full circle. They were looking in and around the woods where our adventure had begun hours earlier, but we were nowhere near there now. Our thrilling adventure was soon to come to a painful end.

We were met by my mum and Andrew's mum and dad outside my house. Andrew went off with his mum and dad. They told him off, gave him a hot meal and, after tucking him up in his warm bed, they told him he could not see me for a while as punishment.

My mother literally nearly beat me to death. I couldn't walk for a week. Then I was locked in the small back bedroom which had only a single bed in it, alone and hungry. On the second day she sent some food up for me. She only let me out to go to the toilet. This went on for four days. Every night she would send one of the boys up with a candle when it got dark. I don't know why there was no light in there, the other rooms had lights in them. By the fourth night I had begun to heal from the beating and I think it was David who brought the candle and the food. I told him I was going to jump out of the window and run away. I ate the food, then tried to open the sash window. It must have been nailed shut or just broken, but I couldn't open it. I cried with frustration and despair. Not for the first, or the last time, I wished I was dead.

That night I made my first real suicide attempt. I took the candle which was stuck to a saucer, held on by melted wax, and I set fire to the curtains. I sat on the bed as if in a daze and watched the smoke slowly turn to yellow flames. I then lay down, watched and waited for the flames to reach me. I never imagined that it might hurt and I hadn't thought far enough ahead to think that it might have burned the whole house down. I just wanted to kill myself. Life was unbearable.

My mother must have smelled smoke. She came in and threw a bowl full of water on the curtains. The flames never reached anywhere near me or the bed. It cost me another thrashing, but then she let me out and I went into my own bed that night.

I wasn't allowed out of the house for a while. I missed Andrew terrifically and I made the boys promise to tell him that I was all right. When I eventually did get to see him he told me that his mum said that the police had told my mother the night that we were missing, that she wasn't looking after us as she should. They must have suspected that we needed the supervision of the social services, but up to this point, nothing was done. This was why she had been so hard on me, they were being found out at last. It would be another year of hell for us children before something happened which resulted in us being taken into care.

That year, me and the boys were to stay in Scotland with Auntie Mary and Auntie Annie. This must have been to relieve

A Saint I Ain't

our mother, who by now must have had her hands full with six lively children. We stayed for two or three weeks during the summer holidays.

Auntie Mary was to stay with us for a while, then me and the boys were to go back to Scotland with her. For what seemed to be weeks before her arrival, mum and me and the boys scrubbed every inch of the house from top to bottom. This was the only time I remember decorating the front room. We scraped all the old paper off with kitchen knives, a slow process which left blisters on my hands. Then dad put on this flowered wallpaper and a border, which had to be cut in long strips I remember. We painted the skirting board and window sills. It took all day and through the night, then dad had to go to work, but it looked good when we had finished. Mum and me made a peg rug to put on the grey stone floor. This rug was simply old potato sacks ripped open and sewn together into a large square, then old coloured rags were torn into strips. We used a wooden peg to push the strips through the holes in the sacking, then back through the nearest hole, leaving a coloured loop on one side and knotting the underside to hold it firm. The result was a mass of bright coloured material, making a strong rug which was hard wearing and would last long after the visit from our Aunt.

When she arrived, I remembered how lovely she was. She was beautifully dressed and smelt as though she had spilled a bottle of perfume over herself. Her hair was ginger like my father's. Her character was not in the least like his however. She was gentle and mild mannered. She didn't drink or smoke. Our mother used to smell of old smoke. When she caught us and pinned our heads between her legs, squeezing her knees together, clasping our head in a vice like grip, checking for head lice, I used to feel sick at the smell of her smoky apron. This lady smelled of lavender soap, not smoke. Everything about her was loveable. She had a lovely smile and we decided that she must be very rich. I know now that she wasn't rich, she was just a working class lady, but she was like royalty to me.

While she stayed, my parents were on their best behaviour.

They didn't swear at each other and he didn't get drunk. He still went to the pub, but he came in sober, something we weren't used to. It felt strangely quiet in the house. Mum told me many years later that it was during this stay that Auntie Mary had asked if I could live with her and they had said no. She also told mum that she should divorce, even though she was his sister. This surprised me. Such a strict Christian lady advocating such a thing must have meant it was more serious than I realised. I am sure she would not take the break up of their marriage lightly. Things must have been noticeably bad at that time. Even then, we children never imagined they would split up.

When her stay was over, Auntie Mary took us back to Scotland with her on the train. I remember Edinburgh station as if it were yesterday. It was so exciting. Then from the train station we went on to Auntie Mary's house in Fife. They all lived within a short bus ride of one another, all my father's brothers and sisters. All three of us stayed at her house the first night. We all had supper together, then we went to bed and fell straight to sleep. For the first night we all slept in her double bed. Tomorrow the boys would go to Auntie Ann's where there was more room. Auntie Mary and Uncle Bob slept on the bed settee on the lounge. After tonight this would be my bed for the rest of the stay. The upstairs flat where they lived had just one bedroom, that was all they needed. The tenement block they lived in had about six flats in each block. All the families shared the entrance and a stone stairway linked each house. They didn't have any gardens. Right outside the back door of the building, past where all the dustbins stood tidily, there was a belt of green grass with a set of swings on it. I spent much of my time playing on these swings. Auntie Mary could see me from her back kitchen window. It felt comforting and warm to see her in the kitchen while I worked my way higher and higher on the swing. Sometimes she would wave to me and I waved back. I wished I could stay there forever.

The front of the tenement block overlooked the street. Each house had a balcony off the bedroom. I loved to stand on the balcony and watch the world go by, no one seeing me there, all busy getting on with their everyday lives.

Uncle Bob was a man of few words and they were an extremely happy couple. He was naturally quiet and she exemplified the prefect wife. He hardly spoke to Auntie Mary so you can imagine how much contact with him I had, but it was never a strained silence, it was wonderfully peaceful and calm.

When my Aunt and I were out together shopping in the high street, she could talk the hind leg off a donkey. She was always laughing and happy and she used to sing while she was cooking and cleaning. This was alien to me. I can never remember my mother smiling, let alone singing. Both my parents used only two forms of communication with one another, and with us. They swore or they hit. If they did speak to each other or to us, they always shouted, adding a light peppering of verbal abuse at the same time at every opportunity.

During my precious few weeks in Scotland, I received such warmth and love from my Auntie and Uncle that it would hurt me to go back to my real home. The morning after we arrived we had taken Robert and David on the bus to Auntie Ann's and Uncle Jock's house. They had two daughters, Susan and Jenny, who were the same age as the boys. Ann was my father's sister too. She was tall and thin, not a bit like Auntie Mary. She was quite sharp and would stand no nonsense from the boys. I was glad I wasn't staying here. They were kind of course, but this big house wasn't calm and quiet like Auntie Mary's. It was a real hive of activity all the time. We arrived as they were making jam in the kitchen, and the smell was wonderful. The boys were told to take their things to the bedroom, then all five of us went out to play. We all got on right away. These girls were fun, not like my little sister back home who cried all day. After an hour or so we found ourselves in the large strawberry patch. We had never had fresh strawberries before. We got a lot of things we had never had while we were on that holiday. Before we knew it, between the five of us, we had eaten the whole strawberry patch bare. Me and the boys must have had most of them because on the way back to Auntie Ann's, we were all sick. To this day I find it hard to eat more then a couple of strawberries without feeling sick.

The luxury of being the only one was indescribable. The flat was an Aladdin's cave to me. She had collected ornaments from all the countries she had visited. Each one had a tale to it. I asked so many questions that Auntie Mary would laugh at me and say, "You'll wear your tongue out." But the sheer pleasure of being spoken to, and of speaking, without being punished in some way for it, was wonderful.

Auntie Mary was the post lady in the town. They called her "Postie", and she had a bike with a big metal basket on it to hold all the letters and parcels. On the few occasions I helped her, I sat in the basket when it was empty and she rode me home. Everyone loved her. There was something about her that made people want to be with her. I was so proud to be out with her. When we went to the shops everyone would stop and speak to her. She had time for everyone. She was a very knowledgeable lady as well. She had travelled the world. Uncle Bob never went on holiday with her. He never wanted to go. She used to say, "Bob dis ne know his way out of Fife. Besides, he has his wee dog te look after."

They liked it this way obviously. She had been to almost every country in the world. She showed me dolls, trinkets and postcards from America, Canada, Israel, China, Russia, you name it, she'd been there. I could listen to her for hours. I could write a book about Auntie Mary, she was such an interesting lady. Alone in the flat sometimes, I examined carefully all the things I could.

Another sad but significant memory of my time at Auntie Mary's is my sheer delight at being clean. I had clean sheets on the bed, I can smell them now. She bought me new underwear so that I could change every day. Wow! The house was clean and smelt of furniture polish. Our house was filthy, dark and smelly. This flat had white paint work, ours had yellow brownish smoke-stained skirting boards and ceilings. The smell I remember most from Auntie Mary's was of baking and cooking; wonderful smells. And the bathroom smelled of scented soaps, bubble bath and hot water. I never wanted to get out of the bath once I'd got in. Auntie Mary would shout, "Come on out Mary, you'll get wrinkles and shrink."

I thought this was very funny. Sometimes Auntie Mary washed my hair for me. It was long and golden coloured. Then we sat in the lounge in front of the television while she brushed it until it shone.

The first day when I went to the swings I met another girl who was also called Mary. She was my age as well. There were few children who used this play area. I think this street had mostly older or single people living in it. Mary lived further up in town but she used this play area to be alone. She, like me, was quiet and reserved. She, like me, had brothers and sisters at home. We became good friends. Sometimes she would come and have tea with me, and Auntie Mary encouraged this. Sometimes I went to her house. Her mum and dad were lovely. They too had about six children, but their house was clean and there was no fighting, and it smelled of food and nice things like Auntie Mary's. Why can't we be like this? I thought to myself.

The rest of the holidays were a happy time. Mary and I even went to the seaside. Then the day before we were due to go home my dad came to take me and the boys back on the train. When it came to bedtime, I was to sleep in Auntie Mary's bed with him and they had the settee in the lounge. I daren't tell her, but I didn't want to sleep with him.

I went to bed as usual and they sat up talking. He and uncle Bob went out for a pint. Late that night I was woken by him on top of me. He wasn't drunk this time, so there was no excuse. I lay awake most of the night. The next day I didn't want to see Auntie Mary, I thought she might know. By now I was nine and I knew it was wrong, but I daren't tell anybody. I think I was afraid he would do to me what he did to my mother. We went home the next day, and life continued the same for us. The next year, during the six weeks holiday, we returned to stay with Auntie Mary. This time we went on our own on the train. This was especially exciting for us. Mum saw us off at the station, and Auntie Mary met us at Edinburgh. Our return journey would be the same. We were old enough now. Again the boys stayed at

Auntie Ann's and I stayed with Auntie Mary. I met up with my friend Mary as soon as I could. Our second holiday was as good as the first, but it would be our last visit to Scotland until we were grown up. From then on we had regular letters and Christmas presents, but we never saw Auntie Mary for many years.

A Saint I Ain't

Chapter 3

It was now 1963 and many changes were about to take place in our household. The boys had shown an exceptional natural musical talent in the secondary school and now they were set to go to college to learn advanced music. They were given a grant towards lodgings, but this money went, as ever, on booze. They had to travel every day by bus to the college. At that time the boys wanted to join the army. They applied and were accepted into the Junior Leaders as young musicians when they were both sixteen. Eventually they were to go their separate ways; Robert stayed in the army where he played all over the world. David left the army and went on to play French horn with many top orchestras.

In September 1963 I started the secondary school. I was beginning to struggle academically now. I'm sure I had the ability to learn more than I did, my mind was alert and I was interested, but the enthusiasm to learn must be nurtured by your tutors and your parents. At home we had enough trouble simply surviving from one day to the next. To have asked for support from our parents would have been met with a negative response. They were already an embarrassment to us when, on the few occasions they had contact with the school. It was usually to complain, or they were sent for because one of us was in trouble. When I sang in the school concerts or the boys played in the school band, they were not there to see us. To get things like sewing materials or cookery items, was a major task. A swimming costume became part of the PE lessons, money for crisps and a drink which all the others had, everything was an obstacle for us. No one will ever know how hard it was to manage to keep our heads above water. As soon as the music teacher learned that I was the boys' sister, he wanted me to join the band. I had never been interested like them, but they had taught me to play. I had never learned to read music but I could play easily by ear. The teacher was very angry when I said I didn't want to join the band. He made my school life hell for a few weeks until I gave in and joined. I began at second cornet and still struggled to read music. I knew it was going to be near impossible to practise playing at home, but the teacher would never know or care.

I was still having a rough time at home. I had little interest in anything these days, I missed the boys so much, and I hated the rest of my family for a while. At secondary school I was picked on even more by my peers who called me names. As of old, I was always in trouble for being late, though on the whole it was easier to avoid trouble in a larger school. I learned all the crafty tricks I could to turn up, get my mark, and avoid handing in any homework I should have done and hadn't, then nip out at playtime and skive until home time, then walk in the house as if I had been to school.

This went on until Christmas, then we broke up for the holidays and I was never to go back. I don't remember much about that Christmas. On New Year's eve we were always allowed to stay up till midnight to see the New Year in. This was a Scottish tradition which even our family kept. Mum would bake cakes and a special recipe called dumpling, a sort of moist pudding, steamed and served hot or cold. It was the only time of the year when she made dumpling. There were cream crackers and cheese, fresh bread and shortbread, trifle and fresh fruit. Tradition has it that whatever you are doing on New Year's eve, you will do all year round, so a full table, laden with fresh things symbolises good things all year. We all had to have a bath and put on clean clothes. Even mum took off her pinny and put a clean dress on for New Year's eve. Dad had gone to the pub but he would have to be back before midnight to see the New Year in all together. He came in and we all sat waiting for Big Ben to strike

A Saint I Ain't

midnight, watching The Andy Stewart Show on television. As it was striking, we all hugged and kissed each other and the party then began. Our father went out the back door, as he did every year, and knocked on the front door. The one who opened it was given a piece of coal by him for good luck, and they then invited him in.

I will never know what led to the fight that particular night, but as usual a fight began between our parents. The little ones ran up to bed and the boys and I looked on. When fights happened during the night, as they often did, there was nowhere to escape to. This New Year's eve we followed the younger ones to bed when our mother told us to. The boys climbed in with Paul and I got into my bed. The noise of the fight progressed from verbal to physical. It was about his drinking. We could make out some of what was being said. He was calling her a lazy so and so and she was calling him a drunken pig. This was a particularly nasty fight we could tell. At some point in the early hours of the morning, we heard voices downstairs. The police had been called and they were shouting at dad. Mum was saying it was all right, telling them to go away, but they wouldn't go. We sat at the top of the stairs listening. The policemen were pushing dad and trying to provoke him into retaliating. They were shouting something about hitting women and not men. We sneaked downstairs and watched through the half-open door. No one saw us in all the commotion. They were making him stand up, then pushing him down on the settee, then shouting at him to stand up, then pushing him down again. He was very drunk. They taunted him, shouting, "You're brave enough to hit a woman, go on, try it with us." He was so drunk that it was having no effect on him. Eventually they gave up and went.

Within a few days another fight began in the night. This time it was even worse. The police came again, then an ambulance and mum went to hospital. This time the boys and I knew it was bad. From nowhere, it seemed, a man appeared in the downstairs room. He was a social worker, but we didn't know this. He came up to our bedroom where we were all huddled on our beds. He spoke to the boys while I tried to stop the little ones crying. Then he turned to me and gently said, "Where's your nightie?" I was wearing one of David's shirts which I always wore in bed. It was ripped and dirty. I didn't have a real nightie but I said to the man, "I couldn't find my nightie so I put this on." I knew by the way he looked at me that he could tell I was lying. He glanced around the filthy room, then at all of us, shivering with a mixture of tiredness, cold, fear and embarrassment. Then he went downstairs. We all thought mum must be dead and even the boys started to cry. This time it was bad.

Mum wasn't dead but she needed stitches from a cut and X-rays. He had nearly killed her this time. He was taken away by the police. Now we were alone with some stranger downstairs who had not told us anything. Soon mum came back from the hospital and they would talk all night. The younger ones fell asleep, but we older ones sat up wondering what was going to happen to us.

The next morning mum told us that me, Paul, Jill and Philip would have to go away until things were sorted out. She said that Robert and David would stay to look after things at home and everything would be all right. What actually had taken place was that she had signed us over to the care of the authorities until she found a safe place for her and us to move to. Our family had now split up. Robert was sixteen, David fifteen, I was eleven, Paul nine, Jill seven and Philip was four. We were not told where we would be taken or for how long. A car came for us mid-morning. We were told to get into the car by our mother. She was crying and she simply said to me, "You are in charge Mary, look after the little ones." She went back into the house in tears. I looked back as we drove off, seeing the boys bravely fighting tears and waving to us. Philip and Jill were crying, and Paul and I held one each, to comfort them. Paul and I grew quite close during our time in care. Up to now it had been the boys and me; now they were to leave us all, mum included. Within a month or two they both went into the Junior leaders, even though David was too young by about nine months. Someone must have fixed it.

The car drove us to a clinic where we were examined by a

doctor. I found this very embarrassing. I had head lice and body lice and was seriously underweight; we were probably all the same. After the examination, we were taken to a children's home where we would live for the next two years.

The home was two council houses knocked into one. It had room for eight children at a time. It so happened that they had room for all four of us. They didn't want to split us up.

The first thing I remember happening in the home was that I was made to get into the bath with my sister. I remember feeling very embarrassed. My sister had never seen me naked before, we certainly had never taken a bath together. The lady in charge, Pat, had taken all our clothes and told us she was going to burn them. I remember worrying that we would have nothing to wear when we got out of the bath - we had left our house just as we were.

In the bath Pat scrubbed me painfully with a scrubbing brush. She pulled my long golden hair, which I had never had cut, and was trying to untangle the mass of knots. She got shampoo in my eyes and soap in my mouth, it was all a very painful experience, physically and emotionally. I just wanted to cover up my nakedness, but she had no sympathy. We were given second-hand clothes to wear when we got out of the bath, Pat remarked in the bathroom that I should have been wearing a bra, not a vest. My breasts had fully developed and I was big there if nowhere else. We were given second-hand underwear to put on. Jill and I were shown to the bedroom we were to share. Paul and Philip were to share a room with two other boys. In our room we had a single bed, a single wardrobe with shelves in it, and a bedside cabinet with a lamp each.

We went downstairs and joined Paul and Philip who were already in the playroom. We were all very quiet. We sat at a table in the dining room. This was the first time we had sat at a real dining table set with knife, fork and spoon, and eaten as a family. We were used to roughing it and eating what we could get at home. It was very rare all six of us were in the same room at the same table to eat together. I had eaten at a set table at Auntie

Mary's but that seemed so long ago now, besides, that was fun and informal. This was uncomfortable and strained. Now we were being shown how to behave at the table by a perfect stranger who, just a short time ago, had seen us stripped naked and had washed and scrubbed me in the bath. It was all very alarming. I remember thinking, I'm not going to like it here. We all sat and ate in silence.

After the meal we went into the playroom which was a large long room, which must have originally been two rooms and now the dividing wall has been removed. At one end there was a large old-fashioned wooden table and in the corner a big cupboard built in to the wall. It was big enough for us all to walk into. In it were shelves, filled up to the ceiling with toys and games such as we had never seen before. It was like a toy shop, attracting even me who, by the age of eleven should have grown out of toys and games, but I hadn't. We weren't really used to playing with toys. On the right hand side of the room, half-way down, were lockers. These were small wooden cupboards about two feet square, all in a row. Each child in the home was allocated one to keep personal things in, plus a key to keep it locked. At the front end of the playroom were easy chairs and a television. It was all rough, but clean and comfortable. Nothing in the room matched and everything looked second-hand. The kitchen was amazing. I had never seen such a large kitchen before.

The first evening in the home was difficult for me. All the other children came in after school and we were suddenly over run with noise and activity. All four of us were stunned from the long night and the even longer day we had just had. Jill and I went to bed early. She fell asleep straight away. I lay in bed confused and over-tired, unable to sleep. It was only then in the stillness of our room that I began to realise the seriousness of what was happening to us. We were in foster care. No one had told us anything. We had been taken away from our parents for our protection into the care of the local authority. My mother had given her permission. She would have had to agree I suppose; we needed care that she and our father were not giving us. I lay in

A Saint I Ain't

bed thinking, so many questions in my head. Where were we? No one had told us even the name of the town we were in. How long would we be here for? Could I still go to the Tuesday Club? Would I ever see Andrew again? Would I be going to my old school? What about the house? Would dad kill mum when the police let him out? What if I never saw Robert and David again? I could see them now out of the back window of the car. She had told me not to cry. You're in charge of the little ones. The day had been so long. I let go and the tears came. It was all too much too soon. My crying would stop though. A new and much harder Mary would leave this place.

The single bed felt strange to me. The sheets were starched, white and clean, no bare damp smelly mattress. I had a pillowcase and a real pillow and blankets instead of old coats. It was not the same here. It was too clean. I had been given a new pair of girls' pyjamas by Pat. I suddenly missed David's old familiar shirt. My belly was fuller than I remembered it being in a long time. And the thing that I missed most was the noise of my mother and father fighting. All the things I should have wanted to see go were the things on my mind now. I wanted them back. As hot tears ran silently down my cheeks, I wanted them more than anyone will ever know or understand. They, to me, were home and security. They were real, this place was not and never would be.

Suddenly without realising that I had slept, there was noise and movement going on outside my room. It was now morning. Someone knocked on our door and shouted for us to get up. A girl a couple of years older than me came in to our room. Her name was Ruth. She showed us to the girls' bathroom. On the way down the landing we passed Paul and Philip in the boys' bathroom. They were being shown how to wash themselves and clean their teeth. They too had new pyjamas on like us. It seemed strange seeing them in pyjamas for the first time. Ruth pushed a new toothbrush into my hand. I was still half asleep because I remember I squeezed the toothpaste out of the tube on to the back of the toothbrush, much to the amusement of Ruth. I was given a new hairbrush of my own. As I said, I had very long golden hair. I would soon be free of head lice and begin to be proud of my hair but at this precise moment I was dazed and still not awake. I asked Ruth what time it was. "7.30," she told me. What? Who gets up at this unearthly hour, I asked myself. I was used to falling out of bed and into school in around ten minutes flat. I went into my bedroom to get dressed. I put on the clothes I was given the previous day.

Down in the dining room for breakfast, I was still half asleep, then I saw Philip and Paul. They looked worse than I felt. All four of us reeled at the speed which these people moved. They were all used to this, we weren't. I hope we don't stay here long enough to get used to it, I thought. The food was good though! Suddenly they were all off to school and left us four at the table. We were told by Pat to go into the playroom. As the morning went on, we woke up slowly. Philip was crying for his mum. He was four and a half and hadn't even started school. Jill and Paul were ransacking the toy cupboard. They were in toy heaven. They got everything out. They squealed with delight at all the toys. Dolls and cars, trains and bikes, games, Lego and Meccano. Philip soon stopped crying and joined them. I tried to keep them under control but I couldn't. Jim, Pat's husband, whom we had met briefly last night and again at breakfast, had been in twice and told them to keep the noise down, but each time after he had shut the door, they began again. Then the playroom door flew open and Jim came in and shouted at us all in a loud angry voice, "Maybe you have all behaved badly at home, well we won't have it here."

He took each one of us one at a time into the hallway and beat us with a clothes brush. Then he left us in the playroom saying, "Sit quietly until I come back." Then he went away. Soon Pat came into the playroom. She gave no explanation as to where we were going. She said, "All of you, get into the car."

Silently we got up and followed them to their car. We drove for a long time. As we were from a family without a car, this too was a new experience for us all. I tried to see where we were going, but soon I was very lost. I was feeling threatened by these people whom we had only met yesterday and who had already hurt and humiliated us by burning our clothes, seeing us naked in the bath, something which even our father and mother had not done, and then, just an hour ago, he had beaten each one of us. What was going to happen next?

We arrived at a large warehouse. It looked like a big shop to me. We were all given new clothes straight from the shelves. There was only us there, and nobody paid.

I received two blouses, a cardigan, a skirt, a dress, a grey pinafore dress with pleats and a couple of jumpers. Besides these things, I was given some shoes, slippers, a coat, socks and underwear, a night-dress and a dressing gown. All the others got all they needed too. The clothes we had on were given to us from a store of second-hand clothes kept in the home for emergencies, these clothes from the warehouse were all brand new.

The journey back to the home was much lighter for us and for them, but I still thought we would be going back home one day. We were driven back to the home. I wanted to stop off and see Andrew and my friends from church. I would miss them. They may never know where I went to, I thought as we drove on past familiar places. I was missing them much more than I was missing my family at that point.

Back at the home, we went to our rooms to try on our new clothes, then to put them away. I must admit, it was nice to have my own bed and wardrobe. I sat on my neatly-made bed in the relative comfort of my own room and I thought of life at home with my parents. I can't remember ever having much to call my own. I mostly wore hand-me-down's from David, mostly his old vests and shirts. All the things Auntie Mary had bought me were now either ruined or lost, or I had outgrown. For school I had a second hand old school skirt and David's shirt. I had one of the boys' old school ties and blazer and I must have looked a sight. I had a couple of dresses for the evenings and weekends, but nothing really fitted me. My shoes for school had cardboard soles in them and my feet were always cold and wet. Out of school I wore plastic sandals. Socks in our house were what might you call communal. You wore what you could find. Socks seldom matched, but you tried to pair them up, then you wore them in bed as well. When the other kids at school bullied us about our clothes, which was often, the boys would fight them in the playground. At home we would get into street fights at weekends and holidays. Who said, 'Remember the happy childhood summers when the sun always shone'? Not me!

At home our bedroom was not nice. Everything in the house was shabby and uncared for. The little touches like lampshades were missing and the curtains in some rooms were little more than rags, pinned up against the dirty windows. There were no pictures on the bedroom walls or ornaments. I had nothing of my own like the other girls I knew. No brush or comb of my own, no jewellery or necklace, no doll or teddy. I never owned a diary. The only watch I had, which Auntie Mary gave me, dad had pawned and lost the ticket, well that's what he said. This is why I treasured the things from the Tuesday Club. All these I had left behind when we were rushed out into a car. They were hidden in an old pillow case under my bed. I would never see them again. We had no privacy at home. With two adults and six children around, there was never quiet in the house. Nowhere to be on your own. There was no order, no rules or discipline in the true sense of the word. Never could the violence and anger which could break out at any time, without warning, be constructive in any way as to help us to grow into mature rational adolescents. In short, we never had a hope in hell of escaping long term problems to some degree.

I remember very little about the first few weeks in the home. Philip began school for the first time. He went to the local infant school. Jill and Paul went to the junior school which was attached to Philip's school. I asked if I could go to my old secondary school but was told no. I would go to the local Grammar school just along the road. My first day at this school was nerve-racking.

For one thing, I knew I would see some of the children from my old junior school who had gained entry to this school by

A Saint I Ain't

passing their eleven plus. They travelled by bus from my old village every day. They would know I was living in the home now and my life would be hell again. Ruth and others from the home went to this school. They were used to being sniggered at by the other kids who whispered, "Those are the kids from the home." I would have to get used to this. It would be a change from "Mucky Mac".

On my first day I was introduced to the class simply as "the new girl". The pupils seemed all right to me. Even the couple in my class from my old junior school turned out to be pleasant and friendly. I was shocked but pleased. They never asked why I was in the home and I never told them.

I found the work in this school very different to my last one. The pupils were much better behaved. The atmosphere as a whole was better. The teachers wore mortar boards and gowns which I found amusing, as I did having to stand when a teacher came into the room. There was much more discipline here. The respect for the staff was evident and the pupils had respect for one another. This was still my first year of secondary school. My last school had more basic teaching standards so I was noticeably behind in all subjects. At first the teachers allowed for this, but I think they put me in a class far above my ability. Maths was a subject I had always struggled in. I never caught on to division, multiplication and subtraction. Now this class was on to algebra and geometry, which I had never done, and I simply could not do it. The teacher knew I was from the home and this meant I may not stay long. Trying to teach me from scratch would be impossible. I was allowed to read during this class. They also did French which I had never done, so again I was left to do anything I wanted as long as I was quiet. Science in my last school was basic too. Here they were much more advanced than I was, but I was able to keep up and learn some things. I had never done biology, but this I picked up quite easily. I wasn't stupid, I simply hadn't been taught all these things, plus I had not been to school much lately. Geography and History were more interesting than my last school. Music I always found easy, but I didn't tell them I could play an instrument. I was still much further behind than the rest even in music. English was always my best subject, here I was as good as the rest.

All in all over the next eighteen months I was left to struggle for the most part. I was never given any homework and most of the teachers never knew my name. This was fine as far as I was concerned. Life in the home became bearable.

Around my twelfth birthday in March, many things began to change. My mother was allowed one visit a month. This was a very uncomfortable time for us all. She used to cry and the younger two did the same. Me and Paul were getting tough. I asked if I could go to the Tuesday Club in our old village now and she told me that I couldn't because I might be seen by our father. She thought he might try to abduct me or something. This meant I couldn't see Andrew either. If he knew where we were he might tell my father. It all seemed stupid to me. I suppose I should have felt sorry for her, but I didn't. She was upset when she saw us, and now she had lost the boys as well, they had gone to the army. She was living in a bedsit in town all alone. One day we had an unexpected extra visit from her. It was to tell us that she was going to divorce the old pig. He was applying for custody of us. That's a laugh! However the court has to be seen to be fair and they allowed him to see us. He still wasn't to know where we were living so we had to see him in a courtroom in town.

Running up to this visit, the younger ones had sleepless nights and were very upset. They were afraid of him. When the day came we were taken by car to see our father, accompanied by a social worker who would be with us throughout the visit. It was the same man who had come into our bedroom at home. We had not seen him since. The visit was very strained. The old pig wanted Jill to sit on his knee, but she wouldn't and cried, climbing on to my knee to join a very tearful Philip, who was clinging to me so hard he was hurting me. Paul refused even to look at his father. I spoke to him and I remember he was sober. I can't remember what we said or how long the visit lasted. I

A Saint I Ain't

remember on the way back to the home thinking that, although I had little love for my mother at the moment, she was better to live with than him. He was of course refused custody of us.

I had become very friendly with Ruth who was about three years older than me. We went to school together. At school she was always in trouble. I knew she and some of the other girls used to steal from the cloakrooms during the breaks and dinner times. Soon she began to give some stolen items to me to keep in my bag until we got home. I was never in trouble so they wouldn't search my bag. I can't remember how it started, but soon I was stealing as well, mostly pencil cases and things from pockets. Occasionally there was money and we would share it between the two of us. Back at the home I kept all my things locked in my locker. Stealing was not something which came naturally to me. The turnips and coal seemed different somehow, picking pockets in the cloakroom was stealing and I knew that it was wrong.

One evening I was called into the sitting room by Pat and Jim. I never realised they had a spare key and went through the lockers. I denied everything, as you do. They told me that they knew I was lying and that the school knew Ruth was stealing. I was to be seen and punished by the headmaster the next day at school. I was sent to his office the next day and again denied everything, but I knew he didn't believe me. He told me that I would be caught and it would be the police that dealt with me not him. I know he was trying to scare me into keeping away from Ruth, but it didn't work.

I began to steal from shops with her and others from the home. I was part of the gang now. We did lots of other things which I knew were wrong. I was threatened by the others that if I didn't do the things they made me do, they would make sure that I was kept in care until I was eighteen. I believed them, so I gave in. My admiration for Ruth had grown so much that what was about to happen seemed acceptable too.

The visits in the night began months after I went into care, they were both unwelcome and terrifying. A hand over the mouth in the dark of the night, then silence, save the inward cries of an ill-treated child. I told Ruth I didn't want them but she answered, "It happens here, it doesn't matter."

One day just Pat called me into the kitchen. She showed me a pair of my knickers that were stained with blood. She asked me if I knew what it was and I said that I didn't. She said, "Do you know what periods are?"

"No", I replied.

She said in a very cold way that my mother should have told me. Then she said, "It will happen every month so when you are having a period, stay away from boys."

That was the sum total of my lesson on periods. She handed me a packet of sanitary towels saying, "You can have these but from now on you buy your own out of your allowance." I went to my room wondering why I shouldn't stand near a boy during a period.

The time in the home was turning to years now. I had joined the local Girl Guides and was enjoying the friendship very much. One of the leaders got a good second-hand uniform for me. I fitted in very well in the guides. I enjoyed being involved in the team work and the games and was a quick learner. I achieved many badges and went on day trips and outings with them. I loved the camp songs which we sang. I was able to take full part because when you are in care, the local authority pay a weekly allowance. We had to save so much in saving stamps but the rest we could do with as we wished. So I had my own money to pay for the extra guide activities. I had stopped stealing from school. It wasn't worth the trouble and I knew it was wrong. I suffered a bit from Ruth, but soon she realised I wouldn't be part of it any more so she left me alone. Ruth and I remained good friends though.

I had tried going to the local Church of England church, but the people in the parish church never spoke to me so after about a month I stopped going. Then I went to the Methodist church. This was better. They made me very welcome. Then, one day I overheard someone saying, "We will have to watch her, she's one of them from the home". Although I did continue for a while, I was so embarrassed as now I knew they were watching me in case I stole something, so I stopped going there too. I would never steal from church.

I still read my bible every day in my room as I had done since the day I bought it out of my allowance money. I knew how to pray because I had learned at the Club and the Sunday School. I had very much missed the friendship of the church people when I had come here to the home, but as time went on, I began to realise that although I didn't have them, I did have God. I had looked for God in the churches I had attended, but he wasn't there. In my prayers I would ask for strength to be brave at night when the visits came. I prayed for strength to look after my sister and brothers. I prayed for my mother and for my father too. I ended my prayers every day with The Lord's Prayer. I soon found comfort in prayer, and answers through scripture. I wasn't old enough or indeed wise enough to understand what personal faith was, but I was in fact finding it all on my own.

One night during my prayer time I had a vivid and real experience. I had said The Lord's Prayer and put out my light. As I lay in the dark I felt an overwhelming sense of peace. This was something that had never happened to me before. My mind was filled with God's Presence. I knew He was with me. I remember saying to God, "I know you are with me, thank you for being here."

God said to me, "Yes, I am with you now and I will never leave you."

I was not afraid and it was lovely. It never happened to me again, but I truly believe it was God showing Himself to me because he knew I needed Him. My prayer life and my understanding of scripture were unbelievably changed from that day. I know now that God had given me his Holy Spirit.

Not much changed in the home; it got no better, no worse. My self discipline was stronger and I tried hard to remain fairly strong, but at times this was almost impossible.

When the time came for us to return to our mother, even though I wanted it, this was not easy. I would miss my new friends at school as well as the Girl Guides, and Ruth too. She may have been a bad influence on me, but I would miss her most.

Chapter 4

Our new home was hard for me to adjust to at first. The actual house was clean and tidy and this was a start. Communications between me and my mother were not good and would never improve much. Once again the younger ones slipped back into things much more easily than I did. I tried to talk to her, but my mother was too wrapped up in the recent divorce and house move to care about my thoughts and worries. This move was to be a new chapter in our lives. Mum did try hard at first to make up for the past. We began to celebrate Christmas now and we ate family meals together. We bought one another birthday presents. These things may have been normal for most families but they were not for us.

Two people re-entered our lives again. One was Sandy our little terrier cross who, as his name implies, was a small sandy coloured mongrel dog whom we had for as long as I can remember. Everyone loved Sandy. Anyone who had a dog as a child would say that theirs was the best dog in the world. Well I'm no exception. He was the most popular dog in our last street and here he would be just as popular. This little dog had a character all of his own. He had stayed with neighbours when mum had moved into the bedsit after we went into care. Now he was back with us again. Sandy always had a stone in his mouth. He would drop it at the feet of anyone passing by. When they threw it, he retrieved it with great energy and enthusiasm. He never owned a lead and walked to heel everywhere with us. Back in the last place he must have lived on scraps, but here he had tinned dog food. He never did stray, but now he was content to spend most of his life sitting on the doorstep. It was as if he too realised that a great strain had been lifted from our lives. Sometimes in the evenings when the sun was going down, I would take Sandy for a long walk on my own. I needed time on my own to think and reflect.

I was now thirteen and a half years old. I had suffered greatly during the last two years or so. So many things had happened and at times my mind was unable to keep up with the thoughts which troubled me. Whether it was because of my nature or because I had learned to suppress my feelings I'm not really sure, but either way, I was unable to share thoughts with anyone. Somehow on our walks, I really believed Sandy heard my sad and bitter cries, which I could share with no one.

The second person who came back to us was Andrew. Andrew and I grew very fond of each other during this summer. Mum let him stay at our house some weekends. I wasn't allowed to go to his home because Mum still worried that our father may be around and that he would find us. He never knew where we were re-housed. This was always on her mind. She was afraid of him hurting us, or her. We understood her concerns and rarely argued with her. Andrew and I would go to town together. Sometimes we went to the pictures or to the park for the afternoon. It was becoming clear to us both that we were falling in love. At first this seemed strange, even to us, but we liked it. We never told our parents, but we talked about our future together. We had been friends for as long as we could remember, now our friendship was deepening quite naturally into love. I never told him about my father or about my experiences in the home. Andrew and I were never to know each other sexually. We kissed when we were alone, but he never touched me in an intimate way. He was totally innocent and although I wasn't, I pretended that I was. When he stayed at our house he was treated as one of the family, nobody knew our secret. We were in love and planned to marry. Sometimes when Andrew stayed for the weekend, we would talk about how our family broke up. Andrew had told us that our father had left the house very soon after he had been refused custody of us. All the street had seen what happened. One evening in a drunken rage he piled in the back garden all the contents of the house that he could manage to carry. This included all photos and documents except our birth certificates which mum had taken with her. Then he set fire to them. What he couldn't burn, he smashed in the house. Every one was talking about it. It seemed that even then people didn't realise that there was anything really wrong in our house. This really surprises me when I think about the hell we were living in and no one knew or cared. People wouldn't have known then why he was behaving in this way. In recent years I have met people who knew us as children and they said they never knew he was an alcoholic. After destroying everything in the house, he took to living on the streets in and around the local town. As months turned to years, he became a down-and-out, eventually staying for some time with his sister in Fife, my Auntie Mary, who tried her best to stop him drinking but to no avail. He then went back onto the streets to live in Scotland where he came from. However, as we were starting our new life in a new town about ten miles from our old place, we didn't know where he was, and as he had been more violent recently, we had cause to be worried.

When I think now of my mother, I see how she must have lost all her self esteem and dignity during the years of beatings and humiliation that she suffered at the hands of a drunken bully of a husband. A woman who, now in a relatively safe and comfortable home, was left to pick up the pieces of her shattered life with no support from friends or family. It was inevitable that such damage would have an effect. Never at any time did the social worker give her or us any sort of counselling to help us to come to terms with what we had lived through.

During the first few weeks she told us many things about her life with my father; how they met and about both their families. In the past she never had the time or opportunity to speak to us about anything connected with the past. She was extremely bitter now and spoke with hate and loathing of this man who fathered us. Up to this point I don't think I had any love for him, but listening as we did to the bleak history of their troubled relationship, I had no compassion for him now. I am aware that we only had one side of the story, and this coloured by a bitter lady, but I saw and remembered many of the things that we had all suffered at his hands, and I am still suffering for some of them.

In the silence of my head, I began to have equally little compassion for my mother. I was sorry for her, but why in God's name did she wait until there were six of us to do something about it? It took a fight which nearly cost her life to do something.

Life after the fight was suddenly and abruptly changed. It would never be the same for any of us. Soon the damage to our mother began to show.

Very soon after I settled in to the new house, I joined the local Methodist Church. I began by sitting at the back on a Sunday evening for service. The church people were friendly to me. I was the only young person that attended this service, the rest were middle aged or elderly. I always found it easy to get on with older people. They asked me if I wanted to join the choir. This was a turning point in my spiritual life. I really enjoyed the choir. I went to practices during the week. I was a good singer and fitted in well with all of them. I also joined the choral group which met separately from the church group. We were performing "Merry England". From then on I was accepted fully into the church. I joined the newly opened youth club and made many new Christian friends. I began to teach in the Sunday School.

Sometimes Paul would go with me to church, but he never really got involved like me. My mother began to resent my involvement with the church. Sometimes one of the ministers called at our house. She didn't like this. They wanted her to come to church but she wouldn't. I must admit, they were pushy and she wasn't having it. Methodists do tend to rush in feet first sometimes, well this time it wouldn't work. She resented them and this made it difficult for me too.

The six week school holiday went so quickly and now it was

time to start my third Secondary school. I was quite proud of my new school uniform. Mum was entitled to many benefits as a single parent. This included free school meals and free school uniforms. On my first day I was introduced to my class mates. Now at least I looked smart and clean from day one. No one knew us as "Mucky Macs" or "the kids from the home". This, I thought, was truly a clean sheet. New house, new school, what could go wrong? Well, anyone who has moved schools during the middle of their secondary education will know what was to come. I was never going to be accepted into a peer group. The girls in this class were really hard and tough and they took an instant dislike to me. The boys in the class disliked all girls except their girlfriend.

Only one girl spoke to me from the first day. Her name was Jenny. She was a lovely girl and we became good friends. This was probably because she too was disliked by all the others. I never knew why they hated her so much, they just did and she seemed resigned to this. She told me that she had always been picked on from an early age. Soon I joined the school brass band. The teacher thought I was great. I took up the cornet and was soon second cornet and also played the flugal horn sometimes. I enjoyed playing very much. When the other kids in my class learned that I had not only joined the band, but I went to the Methodist church and I was in the choral society, any chance of fitting in went out the window. They began to make my life hell. So, true to form, I bottled it all up and just got on with it. I was called a "goody, goody bible basher". They teased me and spat at me, kicked and beat me, at school and on the way to and from school. I never told a soul; not the teachers, not my mother. At weekends and holidays they came and picked on me and Paul at home. We stayed in as often as we could. Only Andrew knew. I hated school and couldn't wait till I was fifteen and could leave.

Then at Christmas Robert and David came home on leave. This was the first time we had been together as a family since we were taken into care and the boys joined the army. They seemed to me to have grown into men. They had smart uniforms and lots of money. They went out to the pub a lot. They let me go with them but they never let me have any alcohol. I didn't mind though, I just loved being in their company. They bought things for the new house as well. This house was just a two-bedroomed terraced house in the poorer end of the town. It was right next to a colliery. It was a dirty area next to the coking plant. Outside our door was the railway line which took the mined coal out to the factories and power stations where it was needed. Our street was one of a row of terraced houses. Our front door opened into the living room. This had orange flowered wallpaper which mum had on when we moved in and which remained until the house was demolished to make way for a new dual carriageway many years later. We had a large three piece suite, a television in the corner and an old fashioned sideboard which had two large cupboards and two drawers. This housed all our clothes and socks. There was a large table and six chairs in this room too where we ate our family meals. The fireplace was a large Yorkshire range with an open coal fire and an oven heated by the fire. There was a shelf on which the kettle stood, always filled ready for making tea. By the side of the mantelpiece hung a toasting fork and I can still taste the toast cooked on the open coal fire. The mantelpiece was taller than me. If you wanted anything, mum would say, "Look on the mantelpiece" and, sure enough, any small object you could want would be kept on the mantelpiece. Coins or combs, pens or sewing needles. In the middle of the mantelpiece was an alarm clock. This was always set ten minutes fast so that we were never late. What wasn't on the mantelpiece was on the sideboard. The room was often an untidy clutter but we liked it that way.

Above the fireplace hung a mirror which had a crinoline lady in a flower garden painted on it. These were all the rage then. This room was our main living area. We ate here and watched television here and, as we had no running hot water or a bathroom, once a week it was where we took a bath in front of the fire on a Sunday evening in an old tin bath as they did in the forties and fifties. During the week we used the kitchen sink to wash in.

A Saint I Ain't

Through this room was the kitchen. This was a very small room which had an old cracked sink in one corner around which was a curtain, the purpose of which was to hide the bucket and bowls, floor cloths and sweeping brush. Next to the sink was an old electric cooker. In the oven were kept the few baking trays and pots and pans used for the family meals. Mum mostly used the kitchen range oven to cook stews and pies as well as some cakes and pastries. This too was quite new to us. In the last house, mum never baked and rarely cooked a full meal. Meat and two veg were something you got at school if you were lucky. Now we did have a better variety of cooked meals. Also in the kitchen was a tall cupboard which had a sliding door with shelves on the top. In this cabinet was all the cutlery and crockery we possessed. There was a tiny formica table against the back door where all the food was prepared. Above the table was a shelf for the cups and everyday items which we needed to be handy. The floor was stone and the only covering was a square of lino by the sink. It was all rather dull and gloomy, so small and cluttered that it never looked clean.

To the right of the back door was the stairs. We had a runner on the stairs. This is a carpet which covered the middle of the stairs and protected our bare feet from the cold in winter. The stairs were very steep and, having no window and being no wider than a few feet, they too were dark and gloomy.

The room at the top of the stairs was the main bedroom. Mum made us all use this room together. Thinking about it now, I think she must have felt more secure if we were all together. However, there was no privacy for anyone at any time. We were not allowed to use the bedroom at any time except to sleep there. In it were two double beds, one on each side of the room, with a mattress on the floor in between. At the foot of the beds was a small wooden table which had been painted white many years ago. On this table were the clothes we took off and under it was the dirty washing. We had no drawers or wardrobe. We did however now have pillow cases, sheets and blankets which were donated as were most of the contents of the house, by the social services to help give us a start. The second bedroom had two single beds in it and another old table. This room was kept made up ready for when the boys came home on leave.

Outside the back was a square garden area. It had no grass or flowers. In the summer it was a patch of hard soil where we played football or cricket. In the winter it was a muddy bog or a sheet of ice where we made slides in the ice. At the bottom of the garden was the outside toilet. This was continually frozen up from late summer onwards. We had to unblock it with kettles of boiling water. It was a smelly hole with a wooden door behind which, on string, we kept a fresh supply of torn up newspapers which were cheaper than toilet rolls but not nearly as soft.

In the first few months, mum made a real effort in the house and we all tried to keep the place decent. Having said this, it was not a place to which I would invite friends. Then into the next year, mum was told by the doctor that she had angina. He told her to take things easy and to sleep late if she could. She must have been around her late thirties now but she looked and acted much older. Her hard life was beginning to show. She must have found the quiet life difficult to accept I suppose. She began to stay up all night and sleep during the day when we were at school. In the night she would clean and sew or sometimes bake. I never saw my mother read a book or do anything remotely resembling a hobby. She had probably lost all interest in herself years ago. My father must have knocked it out of her mentally and physically I suppose. We kids didn't think to notice at the time. I resented her being in bed all weekend though and throughout all the school holidays we saw less and less of her. Over a period of a few months, she would spend more and more time in bed, eventually only getting up around eight o'clock in the evening when it was time for us to be getting ready for bed. We all soon got used to fending for ourselves once again.

The house began to deteriorate into a dirty hole again like the last one. The only shopping done was for food when we had collected the family allowance on a Tuesday. Mum signed the book for us, as eventually she never went out. She did perk up a bit when the boys came home on leave.

As I've said, we all shared one bedroom. Mum and Jill had one double bed and Paul and Philip the other. I had the mattress in the middle as my bed. Each time they came home on leave, the boys would drink vodka in their room at night. Mum never seemed to care. They were men now. They were never loud or abusive, just merrily drunk. I couldn't wait to leave school and home.

As I approached fifteen I began to think of what I wanted to do when I left school. Most of the girls in my class got jobs in the local sewing factory. A couple went on to learn hairdressing or to work in shops. Nearly all the boys had apprenticeships to go to. No one that I remember went on the dole. I had always wanted to be a nurse. Now I would have to wait until I was eighteen to be a student nurse. I wanted to get a job where I could live in. I saw an advert in the Evening Star for a mother's help/nanny in Derbyshire. This could be an answer I thought. I told my mother and then I wrote and applied for the job.

Within weeks I heard from the lady. She said that she wanted to come and meet me to see if I was suitable. She gave us a telephone number to contact her. My mum rang from the phone box at the top of our street. I thought that once she saw the house and our family, I had no chance.

When the time came for her to come, we all made a great effort in the house and it looked fairly decent. She drove to our door in a really posh car. She was very polite and spent some time in our front room asking me about myself. I showed her my headmaster's reference which showed me as an exemplary person although academically I was not brilliant. I told her about my involvement with the church and youth club and about the choral society. I told her about my wish to be a nurse when I was eighteen. She said that would suit her fine as her little girl Emily would be going to boarding school in three years time when she was eleven. She gave me the job there and then and told me that I was to start on the Monday after I left school. I was elated.

Soon things began to look better again. I would be sorry to leave my church friends once again and I also felt very sorry for Paul, Jill and Philip who would have a difficult time without me, I knew. But I had to leave as only I knew why. Andrew and I saw as much of each other as we could before it was time for me to go. We agreed to write to each other as often as we could. We spoke at length about our secret plans to get engaged. I would miss him terribly, but I had to go, otherwise I would go mad. We exchanged photos and a few private momentos.

Chapter 5

On Sunday evening I lay awake in bed. My thoughts wandered from excitement to fear when I realised that the time had come for me to leave home. Memories of past hurts were far from me now. The real reasons for me having to get away from my family had no meaning at this moment in time. I had long since forgotten the things my father said and did and I blamed neither he nor my mother for the family splitting up. I just told myself that leaving home was part of growing up. Tomorrow I would go away to work. I had liked and trusted the lady who came to our house and who had given me this job. I knew that I could only benefit from this experience of living and working with a new family.

The next day I was on my way to Derbyshire by bus. I was transfixed as I took in the sights before my eyes. I will never forget the rugged and beautiful landscapes that I saw from the bus window. At the end of my long journey, I was met by Mrs. Stevenson. It was less than a ten minute journey in her car to her home. We drove over a small stone bridge with a stream trickling under it and into the village. On my right was the village green. Here I would watch cricket during the summer months. On the left was the main street. I could see the village church built in the same stone as the bridge and most of the houses in the village. I had never seen such a village in real life. This truly was to me a scene from a picture postcard or the television. My limited travel experience began to show. It never occurred to me then that my family and lifestyle was so vastly different from that of an upper class family. If it had, I would have turned around and gone home right then. As it happened I was so innocent that I was not in the least afraid or apprehensive. I never for one moment thought that I was of a lower class to these people, which I was indeed, but I simply took them at face value and expected them to do the same with me. The car turned up the hill to the outskirts of the village. There I got my first glance of the house which was to be my home.

After she had parked the car in the garage, Mrs. Stevenson took my small brown suitcase out of the boot and we walked together to the front door. I had never seen a private house so close up in my life. Thinking back now, although I was from a very poor background, most of the kids in my school would have probably never have seen such a house either. We were all from working class families and this was no average house. It wasn't the largest house I was to see during my stay with this family, but to me it was wonderful. We went in the front door. It opened into the small hallway with the stairs directly in front of us. Looking up the stairs I saw oil paintings on the walls and a deep Axminster carpet covered the stairs and hall. To the immediate right was a closed door and also to the left was another closed door. We walked together on the left down a passage and into the biggest kitchen I had ever seen. Mrs. Stevenson told me to put the case I was still clutching by the door. I put the case down and stared with amazement at the room I was standing in. It was as big as the whole of the downstairs of my mother's house. It was fitted along the back wall where we were standing with dark stained pine cupboards and drawers from floor to ceiling. Down the right hand side of the room was a large double hob with a string of brightly polished copper utensils hanging above it. Next to this was a door leading to the dining room. From there to the end of the room were drawers and kitchen cupboards, all in the same dark pine. At the far end of the room was a double sink unit next to which was a third sink on its own with a waste disposal in it. Over the sink was a large window out of which was a breathtaking view of Derbyshire. I wouldn't have noticed the

A Saint I Ain't

washing up if I was standing at this sink, I thought. On the work surface next to the sink was a dishwasher. I had never seen one before. All along the left hand side of the room were worktops which had every conceivable kitchen gadget you could name, ending with a large built-in oven unit, next to which was another door. The middle of the room was filled with a massive table in the same stained wood as the cupboards, around which stood a variety of stools and chairs, all similar to the table. The floor was parquet and this set the rest of the room off in a very stylish manner. This room would be a very popular place for me, I just knew.

Mrs. Stevenson led us through to the dining room on our right. This was another very large room. It seemed longer and narrower than the kitchen. The centrepiece of this room was a dark mahogany table which had six chairs on either side and a carver at each end. The chairs had carved patterns on them, all highly polished. Down the right hand side of the room was a matching sideboard. On this stood a beautiful silver candelabra and other pieces of silverware. On the left was a full floor to ceiling window, again overlooking the hills of Derbyshire. This window was hung with a set of velvet curtains which remained shut at most times. There were oil paintings on the walls and a stag's head which I never liked. There was also a display cabinet with stuffed birds and some birds' eggs in it. There was a small window at the end of the room, overlooking the front of the house. The floor was of polished wood, with an embroidered rug in the middle. I looked up to the ceiling and admired the chandelier from which hung a number of lights. The room as a whole was a very elegant dining room and in very good taste; a room that I knew I would never eat in, that was for sure. Mrs Stevenson and I went back into the kitchen, then straight across to the door next to the wall oven. This opened into the washroom. This room was like a launderette with a Bendix Automatic washer and a giant clothes drier next to this. I had never seen an automatic before. They were still quite rare in the average household I think. The rest of the room had all the things needed for laundry as well as an area for ironing, and a clean white sink with brass taps. It had a clothes airier hanging from the ceiling. The room was clean, but not well decorated like the others I had seen. At the very end of the room was the door leading to a kind of greenhouse area where gardening equipment was stored. Through this was the back door into the garden.

We walked back through the kitchen and down the hallway to the stairs. Upstairs to the right was the playroom. This was to be where I would spend most of my time both working and when I was off duty. The room was a large square room with a double window opposite the door where we were standing. Once again I was struck by the wonderful view from this window. We seemed to be very high up into the hills, this was because the house stood alone on top of a hill. Under the window was a table and two chairs. On this table Emily and I would have our meals, and at other times Emily would use it to read or to write at or just to play with her toys. On the floor near us stood a big doll's house all neatly set out with furniture, then some shelves piled high with games and toys. In the corner next to the table was an open toy box which was full of Lego and other kinds of creative building bricks. To the left of the window was a dapple grey rocking horse and above this was a book shelf which seemed to me to have on it as many books as we had in our infant school classroom. There were cushions and small stools scattered around the polished wooden floor. We were still standing at the door, and looking immediately to my left I saw a recess in which was a sink and a small work surface and a cupboard below and above the sink.

"This room is where you and Emily will have your meals," Mrs Stevenson explained. She opened the top cupboard to reveal breakfast cereals and other dried foodstuffs, all we would need for light snacks as well as the all important vitamins and minerals, laxatives and other preparations which Emily had to take to balance or supplement her diet. Her daily regimen was pinned to the cupboard door. Poor girl, I thought. The bottom cupboard had crockery and cutlery as well as pans, etc, and a shelf on the side of the sink held cleaning materials. On a small bracket on the wall in the very corner was a television which Emily was allowed to watch with restrictions on certain programmes and these were written on a sheet pinned nearby.

"This will be your sitting room in the evenings," I was told.

Looking around once more, this would suit me fine, I thought. We walked through the playroom and through a door, down two steps and into Emily's bedroom. This was by far the smallest room I had seen so far. It was a lovely room with a deep pile carpet which was pink in colour and into which I felt my shoes sink. The room was oblong in shape with a tiny window at one end. Along the far wall was a complete white fitted wardrobe unit. Mrs Stevenson opened this to show me all the colour co-ordinated day clothes, including matching shoes, which Emily had for each day of the week. These she would change into when she took off her school uniform, of course. In the sixties only children who attended private prep school wore uniforms.

There were coats and hats too, hung neatly in line. There seemed to me to be enough clothes for six children here. In the matching drawers were play clothes and underwear. Each vest and pants set had the day of the week sewn on a label inside the garment so that she knew that she had clean on each day. There was another drawer full on accessories such as hankies, gloves and scarves. On the opposite wall was Emily's bed which had Peter Rabbit covers on it that day. On the walls were children's pictures and on shelves were ornaments and gifts from all over the world. Included in these were a set of Russian Dolls which I admired from the moment I saw them. At the bottom of the step from the playroom was a dressing table and mirror to match the wardrobe, and a little stool.

I was enthralled with this room and thought of my mattress in between two double beds which had no privacy at all. How lucky this little girl must be I thought, to have a room like this all to herself. This was the first time I had thought about Emily as someone that I was employed to look after. I began to think about what she might look like. What would happen if we didn't get on? Oh, dear, had I done the right thing coming here? This was all very much outside my experience. I was one of six children. I was from a broken home and I had a narrow and limited view of life, family or otherwise. I was suddenly nervous and afraid. Could I cope with caring for a child not much less than half my age. Mrs Stevenson led me through Emily's bedroom to my room.

This room was larger than Emily's bedroom. It had a single bed, a bedside cabinet and a single wardrobe and a set of drawers. There were no pictures on the wall, it was just a plain room, but I liked it and felt comfortable in it. There was a small window which I peered through at once. There it was again, on every side, the lovely view of the Derbyshire hillsides. From my room I could see sheep grazing in the fields. My fears disappeared at once and I wanted to stay there forever. Mrs Stevenson explained to me that she had ordered a uniform for me which had not arrived yet. I hadn't thought about a uniform.

We went up two steps through the door on the left which led directly into a bathroom. Mrs Stevenson told me that this was mine and Emily's bathroom. Wow, I thought. My very own bathroom. What luxury. I was imagining the tin bath by the fire on a Sunday evening and the kitchen sink mid-week. Wait till I tell the kids at home that I have my own private bathroom. I would have to write to Andrew. My mind was racing now. I could see on the shelves scented soaps, real hair shampoo and many other toiletries which we did not have at home, having no bathroom.

I wonder now, on reflection, if Mrs Stevenson, who had visited my home to meet me, had given me the job to give me a small share in the good life which they obviously had. She must have known that we were a very poor family with little or no luxury in our lives. She must have considered that I was capable of handling all this. At this point, however, I never thought of these things.

Through the bathroom and we were back at the top of the stairs. Mrs Stevenson pointed down a wide corridor and said the door on the right was her bedroom. This was out of bounds to me, she said. The room on the left was the guest room. We went back downstairs and into the kitchen where she made us a cup of tea and she explained my duties to me in more depth.

At around three o'clock she said we would go to school to pick up Emily. Emily was a day pupil, at private school which accepted boarders and day pupils. She would begin to board there when she was older but for now she went every day. The school was about twenty minutes drive from the house. We sat in the car and waited for the children to come out of school. As the first few started to appear I began to feel nervous. Would she like me? Would I like her? Would she be loud and precocious or quiet and shy? I wondered if she, like me, may even have been a little nervous too. They came out in groups of threes and fours all laughing and giggling together. They all wore identical uniforms, grey blazers with a maroon trim, grey pleated skirts and grey hats, dark tights and black shoes. This was something I wasn't used to. Where I lived, only the secondary school children wore a uniform. I had never seen younger children wear uniforms.

I was looking out through the car window when I caught my first glimpse of Emily. She came out of the school gate with another girl her own age. They waved good-bye to one another and Emily climbed into the back seat of the car, saying hello to her mother.

"This is Mary," Mrs Stevenson said as we drove away towards their home. Emily smiled at me and said hello, quietly and politely to me. She then began to chatter to her mother about something that had happened at school that day. I was looking at her through the rear view mirror. She had a tangled mass of mousy coloured hair, short, without need of a ribbon or anything to keep it in place. She was slightly built with a slim face. Quite pretty and at the same time perhaps a little on the tom-boy side. She never sat still all the way home. Quiet she was not, neither did she seem spoiled or precocious as I worried. I liked her at once. My nervousness eased for the moment.

When we arrived back home, Emily ran upstairs to the playroom. I went into the kitchen with Mrs Stevenson. She told me that tonight she would prepare the tea for Emily and me and I was to take my case to my room, then join Emily in the playroom and spend some time getting to know her. I did just as I was told without saying any more.

In the playroom for the next hour or so we talked, laughed and played as if we were old friends. Emily had a head start on me. I soon learned that I was her third or fourth nanny. Over the coming weeks and months I would hear all about my predecessors at great length from Emily, her mother and from the daily help Mrs. T.

Mrs Stevenson brought us sandwiches and we continued to get to know each other until around six. Then I bathed her and she got ready for bed. Then I met Mr Stevenson for the first time. He and his wife came into the playroom. Emily's face lit up when she saw her father. She was obviously very close to him. She ran to embrace him. At the same time Mrs Stevenson introduced me to him. I stood up and said hello. I took an instant liking to him. He seemed even warmer than his wife who, although very nice, did have an air of distance about her. She was always my employer, never anything else. He seemed more relaxed both with me and with Emily. She poured out all of the day's events to him in a rush of excited chatter and laughter.

All four of us went into Emily's room. This would be a formal evening routine every night unless Mr Stevenson was working away, which was very often, then it would be just the three of us. Emily would get into bed and Mum or Dad would read a story to her while we all sat together. Then she said some prayers. Then they both kissed her goodnight and we left her to settle down to sleep. I would go to the playroom to tidy up, wash up and do any outstanding jobs before settling down to watch television or read. Sometimes I played with the Lego and other toys just for fun. Then Mrs Stevenson would call me to collect my supper from the kitchen, which she always prepared, and I would take this to the playroom to eat, then wash up there, then go to my room to read, or to write to Andrew.

Every night before I went to bed, I would read my bible and say my prayers. Talking to and listening to God was a very important part of my life, and had been for years by that time. Sometimes I would look out of my window and see the wonderful picturesque view outstretched before me. "How can anyone look at this and not see God in it," I would say to myself. To me God is in nature and in animals. I love the pure and simple things which make up life. Seasons of the year, trees and streams, the sea and the sky. I had not forgotten the night not so many years ago when God came to me in the children's home when I was deeply distressed. I still remembered the feeling of his presence vividly. The feeling of love and peace which I believed he was offering me, I now recaptured in the scenes of beauty all around me in this place where I was living and working. This is what prompts me to remember him and to thank him for everything he had given me. I never saw my simple bible reading and childlike prayers as "faith", they were things which felt quite natural to me. I knew God was there with me and I spoke to him in this special and very private way because I wanted to, not because I had to. God had chosen to reveal himself to me, I hadn't asked him to!

The work as a nanny and mother's help was easy. I had a daily routine to follow which helped. Within a week of starting, my uniforms - two of them - arrived. I actually liked it. It was a green tartan dress which buttoned from the waist up to a black collar, and had short sleeves. A bottle green apron to wear when I was cleaning, a bottle green cardigan, black tights. I had two of each. For outdoors I had a green gabardine coat and a green beret (which I was told to wear at all times), and two pairs of black leather shoes. Mrs Stevenson turned out to be a strict employer, but I always did what I was told and so I was rarely in trouble. The only thing I tried to ignore was Emily's strict diet which she and I agreed not to tell her mother about. Emily and I got on very well from the first day. I was very happy there. Mrs. Stevenson was a social climber and held exclusive dinner parties, from which I was excluded, except to help occasionally with the washing up. As the weeks went on I would lie in my bed at night feeling exhausted and thinking over everything that had happened since I started work there. I was quite sure that I could do this job.

I felt equally sure that the Stevensons wanted me and that Emily and I would get along very well together. I usually fell asleep almost at once.

The next thing I would hear would be a small tapping on my door and a quiet voice saying "Mary, it's 7.30." This would be my daily call from Mr Stevenson on his way down to breakfast. My day would begin by getting breakfast for Emily and me in the playroom. I then got her up and made sure she was washed, dressed and breakfasted by 8.30 when Mr Stevenson called her to take her to school on his way to work. He was a Company Director and went abroad a lot. When he was away on business, Mrs Stevenson carried out this routine. In all the time I spent with the family, I was always well treated and although I was a servant, I was respected and enjoyed working for them. They had two other regular employees. One was the gardener who came odd days of the week, the other was Mrs T. who was the daily cleaner. Mrs T had been with the family since before Emily was born, I learned. She came around nine o'clock every week-day. She was responsible for all the heavy cleaning and some kitchen work as well as all the washing and ironing, including mine. She also came back in the evening if the Stevensons had a dinner party. They did entertain a lot. I think most were connected with Mr Stevenson's work, others were just for fun. Sometimes I was asked to help with the preparations or with the clearing up afterwards. I never minded.

Soon after I settled in and when we were alone in the house, Mrs T showed me into the rooms which Mrs Stevenson hadn't shown me. The downstairs rooms where Mr and Mrs Stevenson spent their evenings were a large lounge through which was a smaller sitting room which doubled as a study-cum-library. Upstairs was an en suite guest room with twin beds in it. Then there was the Stevenson's bedroom, then through that room was another bedroom with a single bed in it. This I was told was Mr Stevenson's dressing room. He used this room if he had to go out, or return, during the night to or from his trips abroad. He had a large walk-in wardrobe in this room which was fitted with

A Saint I Ain't

drawers and shelves filled with shirts, suits, shoes all neatly sitting in pairs and rows of ties and cravats, which were popular around this time. The wardrobe had full-length mirrors on the inside of the doors. Through this room was the Stevenson's bathroom. This again sticks vividly in my mind as an amazing room. It was tiled from floor to ceiling and had a sunken bath with gold taps. I had never seen a sunken bath before. The whole room was as big as our front room at home. It was luxurious even by today's standard. Mrs. T let me help her sometimes when I had finished my work. We laughed and chatted together and she filled me in on all the gossip about my predecessors and other light family and village gossip. I liked Mrs. T very much. She was the kind of person I would have liked as my mum, I thought. During my short stay which lasted only a bit less than eighteen months, I saw just how the other half live.

I watched cricket on the village green in summer, saw my one and only fox hunt, a macabre sport I believed both then and now. But the pageant, splendour and ostentatious display surrounding the beginning of the hunt has to be seen to be appreciated. I also spent a weekend in London staying at one of the Royal mews, which was owned by a friend of the family who was on holiday abroad. Not many young girls of fifteen could say that. We saw Annan and Chi chi in London Zoo.

All in all it was a very happy and rewarding eighteen months. But the lure of a nursing career drew me to leave my job as a nanny. I saw an advert in the paper asking for people aged sixteen who wanted to gain experience in hospital as Pre-Nursing Students. I wrote off to get more information and then I decided to apply. I was accepted and started as a Pre-Nursing school at the School of Nursing in the September following my sixteenth birthday in March.

I went to be interviewed by a panel of people involved in nurse training. They remarked that my academic history was not of the standard they would have liked it to be, but after further questions and a discussion between themselves as I sat nervously in front of them, they decided to take me on. I asked if I could live in, as travelling from where I lived would put more than an hour on each end of the day for me. They agreed it would be more practical for me to live in and explained that my board and lodgings would be taken from my wages automatically. This would leave me very little money but I wasn't bothered, the pay was of little importance to me, I just wanted to be a nurse. I would begin in September.

I held back for a long time telling Mrs Stevenson that I was leaving. I knew she would be annoyed at me for giving such short notice, but I was afraid she would be able to stop me going. When I did at last tell her she was, as I suspected, very angry with me. She said I had agreed to work for her until I was eighteen and this was when Emily would begin to board. I couldn't argue with her, I had agreed that, and now without consulting her I had gone ahead and accepted entry into the School of Nursing. I felt very guilty and selfish, but I left anyway.

Chapter 6

We were all from very different backgrounds, but the one thing we had in common was the dream of being a nurse. We had three days in college doing class work, and two on the wards. I began at the Children's Hospital on a ward with very sick babies who had been born with Spinabifida or Hydrocephalus (water on the brain). I only assisted the nurses but this was enough to gain a tremendous amount of experience. I then went to the Dental Hospital where I worked in the photography department. Here I had my only experience of the operating theatre. I went with the photographer into theatre to get photos of a patient undergoing surgery to remove a tumour on his jaw. After my initial sleepless night with worry that I would faint or something, I emerged confident that I had watched an operation and hadn't fainted. In fact I never took my eyes off the procedure. I would never go into theatre again. At my third and final hospital I worked on the main Renal Dialysis Unit. This was really interesting.

The house where I lived had around fifteen pre-nursing students in it. We were all girls at varying stages of our training. We had a large communal sitting room which had a very old television in it and lots of old easy chairs and a couple of settees. I only went in there to watch Top of the Pops once a week. There was only one bathroom on each of the three floors. Most of the rooms were shared. I had a room with three other girls. We each had a single bed, a single wardrobe and a bedside table. With the exception of one or two, we all got on well together and were friends. We lived in from Monday to Friday and had to go home at weekends. I never spoke to anyone about my past. They all saw me as a nice, friendly girl who got on well with everyone, worked hard and kept her private life to herself. Many of the girls confided in me, they found me easy to talk to, but I never disclosed anything about myself or my family to anyone. There was no need. They saw me as happy, so happy I was.

Our room was on the bottom floor next to the lounge. Each evening we all piled in with tales of our day on the ward. When we were in school we saw little of one another, so there was always something to talk about at home. The terms were divided much like school terms and we covered various subjects which included a great deal of medical learning including anatomy and physiology and first aid as well as instruction on hospital procedures, which was very useful. We had Maths which I was always behind on. This dealt with the medical side of maths such as drug dosages and body temperature, weight, blood pressure, how to calculate these in relation to illness. In theory I understood, but I found calculation difficult. We had science, English and domestic science. Once a week we went to another college where we did one lesson of art, drawing and calligraphy. I was never good at drawing, and if I learned any calligraphy, I've forgotten it now. After art in the same building we had a period of one of many choices of physical exercise. I went to trampolining. I really loved this and did it very well I might add.

So as you see the three days in school were varied and interesting. The wards were hard work, but it was a chance to put into practice what we learned in school. We would be well prepared to begin nursing at eighteen. We had little homework so our evenings were mostly free. Our pay was taken up in board and lodgings and on our bus fare home at weekends. Myself and half a dozen others went ice skating most weeks. Once again this was something I was good at. Sometimes we went next door to the ten pin bowling alley as well. Some evenings at home we would get all giggly and play practical jokes on one another. All harmless fun, but we were mischievous and got up to some pranks. Living in the house, supposedly to control our behaviour, was a sister who had a single room on the second floor. If we got too noisy she would come to the top of the stairs and shout at us. We would then quieten down.

One of the girls in my room was often more boisterous than the rest. She was known to get into trouble in school as well and was sometimes told off on the wards. She got on great with us, but, looking back, I think she had difficulty accepting authority. One evening we were all noisier than usual and sister had shouted at us more than once. We all sat on our beds a bit disgruntled when our friend, who was annoyed at being told to keep the noise down, decided we should get our own back on sister. She got a large piece of paper and on it wrote "BOG OFF" in large letters. She then went quietly upstairs and pinned this to sister's door. All was quiet for an hour or so then she must have come out to the bathroom and seen the note. There was a deafening yell from above. She was demanding to see the girl who had done this. We all giggled in our room. The shouting continued however, ending with the all too serious threat of punishment for the whole house if the perpetrator didn't own up within the next half an hour. Suddenly it wasn't funny anymore. She was really angry. The trouble was, this girl was on a final warning from school and had been told that if she was in trouble again, she would have to leave the home and travel each day to work on the bus. She lived as far away as I did, so this would be very difficult. We decided that as we all were in fact party to the prank, and all of us had found it very funny up till now, one of us would take the blame so that she wouldn't get thrown out of the home. Guess who drew the short straw? Yes, me. I had always been quiet and had never been in trouble in the eighteen months that I had been at college. I agreed to say that I did it.

The whole house waited with bated breath. We had never seen her so angry before. There was silence as I went upstairs and knocked on her door. She opened the door and told me to come in. She shouted angrily at me for a while then told me that I would be seeing the principle in the morning at college. Sure enough, I was called in the office the next day and severely reprimanded. Then, the worst any of us imagined, I was told I had to leave the home at the end of the week. I was devastated. It was no good being annoyed with the culprit, she felt bad enough already. I couldn't own up to my dishonesty now, so I accepted the punishment and had to bus to work from then until I finished college.

Sometimes, in fact many times, I sneaked into the nurses' home after college and, with all the other girls knowing, I slept in my bed as usual. The two main problems were that I couldn't have meals so they brought me snacks from supper and breakfast, and the other was avoiding sister. More than once I had to jump out of the window to avoid detection. I would leave that same way, climbing out of the window in the morning so that she didn't catch me. I never did get caught.

Not long after I began Pre-Nursing College, the weekend visits from Andrew got less frequent. I thought this was because we were both working. I never thought anything was wrong between us. We never argued at all and our friendship was so strong that I thought it was just a natural break we were having. Then one Friday I went home to find a letter from him. It said that we were finished and he didn't want to see me anymore. This came out of the blue. I was deeply hurt and cried on and off for weeks. I was still living in the nurses' home of course, so all my friends supported me at the time. My mother didn't seem to worry. She said, "There's more fish in the sea," which didn't help a bit. The worst thing was I had no clue as to why he had finished with me. I tried to see him but I never managed to catch him. It took a long time for me to get over this, but eventually I had to accept it and get on with my life. I was still very happy nursing, so it wasn't too bad. I had plenty of time to work and study to take my mind off him. It was about twelve months before I was really over Andrew.

Other than losing my friendship with Andrew and the unfortunate incident in the nurses' home, my two years as a pre-nursing student were very happy ones. I enjoyed the work and, although we had very little money, we were able to have a good

A Saint I Ain't

social life as well. I never bothered about a relationship after Andrew, I was happy to work and study. We all were now reaching the time to take the exams and interviews to be accepted as a State Enrolled Nurse (SEN) or a State Registered Nurse (SRN).

When the time came I failed my entry exam as an SRN because, predictably, my maths let me down. The rest I passed with no problems. No matter how many attempts I had to improve, I could never pass the difficult maths exam which would allow me one day to go on to be a staff nurse or a sister. I was satisfied with passing to start the SEN course though.

I started my training as a Pupil Nurse. I have never been as proud as I was when I put on my nurses' uniform and walked onto my first ward. Once again, as in Pre-Nursing College, we did periods on the wards, then some weeks in School. I enjoyed both just as much. I got on well with my fellow students and with the tutors. Now we did have homework which took up most of our free time. We worked very long hours on the wards including months of nights and some split shifts. These were days when we began around 6.30 am and worked until lunch time. We had time off until around 5.30, then worked again until 10.30 at night when the night shift came on. We dreaded these shifts. Sometimes if we had three or four split shifts in a row it made us physically exhausted and we were likely to make stupid mistakes. The ward sisters were very strict with us. They were to be feared. If the sister took a dislike to somebody, which happened to me a couple of times, they made life hell. We were still very young and had little time off. In the spare time we did have, we studied for the end of first year exams. There was little time left for any social life and I rarely went home.

Life at home had changed little in the years since I left at fifteen. The cleanliness of the house, and of my younger siblings had deteriorated rapidly. My mother continued to spend a large proportion of her life in bed. The children were suffering as a result, but no one seemed to notice or to care. David and Robert were still in the army and it looked as though Paul would do the same when he left school.

I passed my first year exam and began as a second year student nurse. Nursing had turned out to be everything that I had thought it would be. I found it very rewarding work. It was hard work emotionally too. Some of our patients came in very ill and were cured. Treatment was often long and sometimes painful, but it was good to see them walk out with their grateful families. Others came in for fairly minor procedures and again, usually went home well. The death of a patient however had an effect on everyone. The doctor always had the job of informing the relatives of a death, but it was the nurses who cared for them after. This never got any easier no matter how often it happened, what the cause of death was, or even how old the patient was. Every death to us was a difficult thing to handle.

My relationship with God was very deep now. I would speak to him in prayer most days. I asked him to care for the people who were ill and my fellow students and nursing staff. Situations which I found difficult to handle I always prayed about. I know this sounds corny but I really believe that God helped me to be a better person. The things which I read in the bible I could relate to myself and they were my personal yardstick, if you like, for my daily behaviour. I never discussed religion with my friends and I never went to church, even when I did get home. But I was living a strict Christian life which only me and God knew about, and it worked for me at that time in my life. Our evenings and time off during the day were spent in the nurses' home. As when I was a Pre-Nursing Student, we had a certain amount of fun, but much more study time. The work was much more demanding too. I have been known to have been in charge of a whole ward during some night shifts when the qualified staff went on their breaks. Even for an hour or so, this was a great responsibility.

There were only four of us who had remained together from the beginning of our Pre-Nursing training until we began our training as student nurses; Sarah, who was now engaged to a policeman called Roger and eventually gave up nursing before she qualified, Lisa who is now a staff nurse, another Lisa who I lost contact with, and finally there was a girl called Cindy. I had many other friends, but these four I had known since Pre-Nursing School.

As time went on I became especially close to Cindy. She had been going out with a boy called Bob for years. Cindy was always encouraging me to get myself a boyfriend but I wasn't interested. She had been trying for a long time to fix me up with a date. At last she wore me down and I agreed to go to the pictures with her and Bob and a boy whose name I can't remember. We went to see "The Graduate", the film which everyone was going to see at the time. I wanted to watch this film, but my date had other ideas. We sat on the back row and he kept trying to kiss me. I however won and I watched the film. I never met him again. After this disaster I just wanted to get back to my studies again.

Soon Bob and Cindy asked me if I would go out with a boy who Bob worked with. They were both apprentices at the pit and had worked together since leaving school. Cindy had known him at school as well. I didn't want a repeat of the last date, so I said no. Bob rang me and begged me saying, "He is a nice quiet boy who just wants a girl to take to his twenty-first birthday party in March."

They both kept hounding me until I said yes. I found out this boy, whose name was Ray, had a car. I was most impressed. Not many young people had a car in those days. Some had motorbikes, but most had no transport at all. I agreed to go on a blind date with him. We met at the bus station where I was to wait for him to pick me up and take me to a pub where we would meet Cindy and Bob. I liked him as soon as I saw him. He was very tall, slim with thick dark hair. He had a lovely smile and a gentle caring personality. We went to the pub and met up with Cindy and Bob. Towards the end of the evening I confided a secret to Cindy. It was in fact my eighteenth birthday. When she found out, she told Bob and Ray and Ray bought me a brandy and Babycham as a special drink to celebrate. When we went home Ray asked me if he could meet me again. He was the perfect gentleman and I was surprised that he would want to date me again. I said yes and soon our friendship grew. Three weeks after we met it was Ray's twenty-first birthday party. His family had hired a room and put on a big party for him. I went with him and there I first met his mother, brothers and sister and lots of his friends and relatives. They all welcomed me like a member of the family. I really enjoyed the party. Our friendship soon turned to love and another chapter of my life was about to unfold.

My brothers and sister were now growing up and family life was changing all the time. My brother David was now married. Robert married June. Paul did indeed join the army. Jill and Philip were still school age. Jill was reasonably all right but she could be aggressive and angry in a flash. Philip was showing signs of being violent and disturbed.

As a family we grew more and more apart as the years went on. We rarely disagreed or fell out even when we were all at home, but we were not as happy together as we might have been. We all had our memories of growing up and we sometimes found things to laugh about which we shared now and then. But on the whole we never spoke of the bad times of our childhood days. It was as if it had not really been so bad. I had been subjected to the worst possible emotional, physical and sexual abuse dealt out by both my parents, carers and others who entered my life. This was not something to be spoken about, and it wasn't until many years later that I learned that I had not been the only one in my family abused by my father. My sad childhood would have an influence on my adult life too. But at that time as I was maturing into an adult, I was happy and full of expectancy.

Chapter 7

Ray and I spent as much time as we could together. When I met him he was still training to be an electrician at the local pit. He went to technical college evening classes. His four-year apprenticeship ended just before we got married. We soon knew that we loved each other and wanted to be together as much as we could.

It took me some weeks, but eventually I invited him back to my mum's house. At first I would have him drop me off after a date streets away from where I lived. He began to ask about my family. I said that they were a little strange and that the house was usually a mess. He said he didn't care. I knew that he would have to meet them so one evening I took him home. He didn't care about the state of the house and he got on well with my mum and my brothers and sister. He even stayed some nights, sleeping in the boys' room. We would sit up most of the night talking to mum and listening to the trains which passed our house all night long. My mum and the others liked him as soon as they met him.

Ray still lived at home with his mum. He was the youngest of four children. All the others were married. I got on very well with his mum. Whenever I went to his house, his mum was baking. She used to make fabulous cakes. All her friends and neighbours had their wedding cakes made by her. She made other celebration cakes such as silver wedding cakes and Christmas cakes and she had many grandchildren so there was always someone's birthday cake and party buns to keep her in a full time job. She was a good cook too, making jams and pickles, as well as having an active social life. Ray's mum was the kind of mum I could only dream about. She took me under her wing. She taught me how to ice cakes and I picked up many other things about family life, which she would never know she opened up for me. I never told her about my family, or Ray for that matter. Ray loved his nieces and nephews. Sometimes we would baby-sit. That was fun. I had little contact with babies, except the sick ones in the children's hospital. In the summer we went to his sister's caravan on the east coast. She had two small sons. This was the first real experience of a family holiday that I had, not counting the week with 'the runs' in Cleethorpes when I was young. Ray and I went out as often as we could. We saw a great deal of Cindy and Bob, as well as going out sometimes with Ray's brother and his cousins.

When our days off fell together, Ray would pick me up from the nurses' home and we would go for a drive or a drink. Unfortunately these days were not as often as we would have liked. My shift pattern was long, and my evenings were study times. He worked long hours too and went to evening class. As often as I could, I stayed at his house.

Within six months of our meeting one another, we knew that we wanted to get married. We had the blessings of both mothers. It would be much harder on Ray's mum as she relied heavily on Ray now that her health was failing. She had him late in life so she was showing signs of arthritis and she had for many years suffered with migraines.

My work and studies suffered as a result of my involvement with Ray. I would rather be with him, so eventually I gave up nursing with only months to go before I should have taken my finals. But my heart wasn't in it. My love for Ray was greater. My only regret later, was that if I had qualified I would have been able to return to nursing after the children had grown up. But at the time I didn't think that far ahead. We had a big engagement party. Ray has a very big extended family, and all his relatives came. On my side only Mum, Philip, Jill and Paul came. Robert was not on leave at the time, but we would make sure we planned the wedding when he was as he would have to give me away. David had left the army and had been working with various orchestras playing the French horn. He was a gifted player.

So the plans began for our wedding. The first thing we did was to go to see one of the ladies from my old Methodist Church. She told us that we couldn't get married there as the Church wasn't consecrated for weddings. I had never been inside the Parish Church in my town and as Ray knew the vicar of his local Parish church, St Mary's, we decided to get married there. After meeting the priest at the Rectory, we booked 22nd July 1972 to be our wedding day. We decided to have The Queens, a local pub for our reception.

I wrote to my Auntie Mary in Scotland and invited her. She had kept up regular contact with us since Mum's divorce. She had come to stay at least once every year and wrote to my Mum often. Unfortunately she would be abroad on holiday when our wedding was to be but she promised to come and see us when she got back. I was disappointed. She was the only relative I had invited and she couldn't come. She was the one I loved most of all.

We asked Jill who was about fourteen years old if she wanted to be a bridesmaid, and Ray's two nephews aged three and five and his little niece who was five were page boys and bridesmaid as well. A neighbour of Ray's made the dresses for them in a peach coloured material and the boys had blue trousers with white shirts and a red bow tie and a red sash around their waists.

As the time drew near and all the preparations were gaining full speed, Ray and I seemed to see much less of each other. He was working as much overtime as he could get to pay for the wedding. My mother had little money to contribute towards the cost, and neither did his mum. We had it all to do ourselves, but we didn't mind. It would be a wonderful day for everyone.

About three months before our wedding day, Ray and I rented a house. It was a two-bedroomed terraced house with an outside loo and no hot water. It was coal fired which was important as Ray had concessionary coal from work. It was furnished mostly with old furniture from Ray's mum. All we bought new was a bed and a new settee and a chair. The front room wasn't big enough for a three piece suite. Everything else including the bedding and curtains came from Ray's mum and a few bits from my mum. We had been given lots of engagement presents and these all came into use - glasses by the dozen and tea towels.

Both our mums were adamant that we couldn't move in together before the wedding, so it was agreed that Jill would move in with us as we had to start to pay rent straight away. She slept with me, and Ray had a single bed in the other room. I bought a wedding dress, a veil and a tiara from a gown shop in town. Time seemed to fly and when the day was imminent both of us were having last minute nerves. Replies were coming in thick and fast. Nearly everyone we had invited said they would love to come.

The reception meal of a starter then chicken salad and a cold sweet was laid on for the family and those who had travelled far to be with us and Robert had given us a dozen bottles of champagne as wedding gift. The photographer was booked and Ray and I had to go to church for a rehearsal.

The night before my wedding as I was putting on my dress and trying to fix my veil and tiara, I looked at myself in the mirror hanging over the fireplace. In the reflection I saw my mother looking at me with a serious look on her face. "You don't have to do it you know," she said. "It's not to late to cancel." I looked back at her through the mirror. Twenty-five years later I would see my own daughter standing before me in her wedding gown and my deep love for her and the memories of my own happy marriage would bring feelings of great joy and happiness to me. But the night before my wedding revived many hurts and bad memories of the struggle to bring up six unwanted children with a man she loathed and detested. How could she wish me happiness? She had not had any. She was either jealous of the love I had or genuinely afraid that my marriage would end in hatred as hers had. I will never know what was in her mind. Either way, she was bitter. I spluttered out something about being sure it was what I wanted, then I went to bed.

That night I slept very uneasily, tossing restlessly all night. I was thinking about my father, and other things which I thought I had forgotten. I even worried that my father would turn up at the wedding and spoil it all.

I was at Ray's cousin Cath's house at 6.30 the next day for a bath and my hair "do". I had very long, thick, golden hair which Cath said would look great in ringlets. Indeed it did. She also put my make up on for me. Cath made me look and feel wonderful. Cath did Jill's hair as well and she too had a welcome bath before we both went home to get ready for the wedding in the afternoon.

When I finally got home the whole house was in chaos. Everybody seemed to be doing something different. We were all getting changed, helping each other with the final touches. Starched stiff shirts to fasten. The fresh flowers for buttonholes had been delivered. Suddenly the car arrived for Mum, Philip and Jill. They left for the church six miles away. After they had gone, Robert and I sat together, waiting for the car to return for us. We didn't say much. We were both very nervous. I had left my all important "belly buster" of a girdle until the last moment as it was so tight I could hardly breathe in it.

When the car came back for us I stepped out of the door and saw that the whole street and more had turned out to see me go. I waved with both happiness and embarrassment. They all waved and shouted to me. It was all very moving. As the car drove down the road towards the church, I clutched firmly onto my bouquet of pink roses and white lily of the valley with my favourite freesia to give both colour and scent to it, when suddenly I remembered.

"I've forgotten my girdle," I cried to Robert with a giggle.

"Well it's too late to go back now," he said, with little sympathy, and a comforting smile. I had paid five pounds for that girdle and I knew I would never wear it now.

As we arrived at the Church, the heavens opened. Paul, who was an usher, was waiting to open the car door for me and someone put an umbrella over me. Going up the path to the church, I got drenched. The rain eased just long enough for a few photos to be taken outside the church of me and Robert and the bridesmaids and page boys. We all looked very smart I have to say. Then we gathered in the porch. The church looked full to me and I was extremely nervous. I looked into the church and saw Ray and I felt much better. The wedding march began to play and, taking Robert's arm, we walked down the aisle together.

The service was over in no time and, during the last hymn, Ray and I were instructed by the vicar to follow him further up the sanctuary to the high alter which faced the beautiful stained glass window upon which I had focused my attention all through the service. The colours and the figures in the window fascinated me. I still had a strong Christian faith which had carried me through some difficult times over recent years. When I couldn't talk to anyone, I spoke in prayer to God who I trusted had answered me on more than one occasion. He was here with me now as I made my marriage vows to love and honour and obey, for the rest of my life, the man standing next to me who, although I loved him, I really didn't know that well. This was the beginning of a new relationship which we were both excited about, but which could lead to a happy marriage or not. Who could tell? Only God knew. The priest gave us the final blessing then we turned to face the congregation, my knees knocking and Ray squeezing my hand equally as nervous as me as we looked down the church at what seemed to us to be a mile long walk to the porch in the distance. Then the priest placed his hand on my head and announced in a loud clear voice, "I now pronounce you the electrician's mate." The whole church erupted into laughter and Ray and I walked with a smile and a giggle through the church as our families and friends watched us. It was all over. We were husband and wife.

After, there were dozens of photos with every member of the wedding party. My mum wore a blue and white two-piece suit with white shoes and a white handbag. Philip had a brown suit with a waistcoat and he looked very smart too. Then, after some photos with our friends, we got into the black limousine which was waiting to take us the reception at The Queen's Hotel.

It was only now that we saw the cake which Ray's mum made for us. This was, she said, to be her last cake. "I'm getting too old for cakes," she had told us. This would be a special one as her last one. And it really was special. It was six sided and had four tiers. Everyone said how wonderful it looked. The taste was never in question. She should have been a professional baker. She had no special qualifications but her baking was outstanding.

At the reception I saw David and his wife. They had come up from London and gone straight to Ray's house and from there to the church. This was so that his wife didn't see my mum's house. David was, not surprisingly, embarrassed to take her there.

Besides Ray's large extended family and my family many of Ray's work mates and my nursing friends also came to see us married and then came to the evening reception. We spent our wedding night at Ray's mum's house. The next day we would leave on our honeymoon. We couldn't afford a posh honeymoon so we were to spend a long weekend at Ray's sister's caravan on the East Coast. This was wonderful except that the rain which greeted me on arrival at the church followed us on our honeymoon. It rained buckets all the time we were there. But true to form, we newly weds didn't notice the weather. We were so happy that we were finally married. It had been a long year but it had been well worth it. We had a wonderful wedding day which we would never forget.

Within a week we were back home in our own little house. Now we were alone. There was no need for Jill to act as chaperone anymore. My lack of housecraft skills now began to show. Ray patiently taught me much of the basic cooking skills which his mother had instilled in him from an early age but which my mother had failed to school me in. Budgeting and shopping were new to me, but I was good with a Hoover and duster. I was very house proud. I cleaned and polished, ironed and washed all day long. Then I made a meal for my husband to come home to. We would sit together in the evenings like two happy kids. Nothing and no one could separate us. Soon we would have a new addition to our family.

Ray's mum had told us that as soon as we had settled, we had to have Ray's dog Patch. Patch was a faithful border collie, very alert and intelligent and had been Ray's dog from being a pup. He used to know when it was four o'clock and he would wait outside school and walk home with Ray. His mum quite rightly said that as he was Ray's dog and as she was now getting on in years, he would have to live with us. We didn't mind in the least. He was a good house dog and we wanted him.

Just a few weeks before our wedding we had a letter from my Auntie Mary inviting us to go and stay with her as soon as she got back from her holiday. We wrote back and said we would come two weeks after the wedding. We could stay with her from Friday to Tuesday. I could also see all my other aunts and uncles and my cousins whom I hadn't seen since I was about nine years old. Auntie Mary had come to visit us in Yorkshire many times but I had not been to Scotland since I was young. Ray had never met Auntie Mary nor had he been to Scotland before. We drove up overnight in Ray's car and arrived early on Friday morning in Fife, Scotland where Auntie Mary and Uncle Bob lived.

As I look back and think about this special couple I remember the lady who was a regular church attender. She was one of the most loved people in her village. Every time she went out, the shopkeepers and others would stop and talk to her. She was held in great esteem by everyone who knew her. When she introduced us to her friends, we too were given a truly warm welcome in this small close knit community. Uncle Bob was very much the opposite. He too was well liked and respected, but he was a very quiet man. He loved his whippet dog Trixie who he took for many hours on long walks. He liked a pint and a smoke and a gamble on the horses or the dogs. She didn't drink or smoke and went out only to her church meetings. They were a very happy couple though, complimenting one another to make a very strong relationship. They couldn't have any children but they spent a great deal of time looking after my cousins, most of whom I had not met yet.

The first day of our visit to Scotland went very quickly. It was funny to watch as Ray tried his very best, usually without success, to understand my aunt and uncle's strong Scottish accent. They in

A Saint I Ain't

turn couldn't understand a word Ray said as he spoke in his thick Yorkshire twang, which even I sometimes found difficult to follow. I had to translate what he said to them, then what they said to him. It would take longer than the three days we had for all of them to communicate without missing one or two words. But even though they were having this difficulty, Auntie Mary whispered to me that evening, "You've picked a good wee man there hen," and he in turn agreed in private to me that all I had said about this lovely couple was not exaggerated - they were very easy to get on with. Ray had been nervous about meeting my family in Scotland. I, in a way, was just as nervous. I had not remembered most of my other aunts, uncles and cousins, and all of the next day we would be visiting some of my relatives whom I had not seen since I was about nine years old.

We went to bed quite early. It had been a long drive for Ray and we were both tired. At first I couldn't sleep. I had a bad night tossing and turning, remembering the night long ago when I slept in this very bed with my father. Now I was lying next to my husband. What would he think of me if he knew? I could never tell him. I knew it didn't matter now, but the memory was still there. It would haunt me forever.

The next day, me and Ray with Auntie Mary went all over Fife from one house to another. Everyone had bought us wedding presents. Each member of my family greeted us with warmth and a full table. We had to eat at each house. We had brought the wedding photos with us and we showed them with pride to everyone in turn. I met cousins whom I had never met before. They all welcomed us both with deep affection. It was very moving for me.

At last by tea time we had done the rounds of all my father's side of the family. No one mentioned my father all day. It had been nearly ten years since my mother and father's divorce. It was obvious to Ray and me that these people liked us despite the family splitting up. We arrived back around six o'clock that Saturday evening. Auntie Mary, not wanting to waste a moment of our short time together, suggested that the three of us went to the pictures in the High Street. After a quick cup of tea (no food - we had eaten enough to last us a week), we got our coats on and walked the short distance up the street to the cinema. We looked at what films were being shown that night. Without realising what it was, and thinking it was a comedy, we decided to see The Confessions of a Window Cleaner. We went to buy a ticket at the box window and the lady one duty said with a grin to my Auntie, "Dinny bother ta pay Mary, in ya go all o yi."

Then a man with a torch showed us to our seats saying, "Are you sure ya want this film Mary?" and he chuckled as he left us. Much to our embarrassment, and the giggles of our strictly religious Auntie Mary, we realised that this was a rather rude comedy which, after the first ten minutes or so, we decided was not for us. The usher doffed his cap to us and the lady behind the ticket counter shouted a quick, "Goodnight Mary" to us as we hurried outside and all three of us burst with a tremendous laugh as we realised why they had not taken our money. It was not the kind of film you take a sweet little old lady to. She saw the funny side and made us promise not to tell Uncle Bob. "I'll never live it down," she laughed as we walked towards her flat. She then suggested another big mistake, "Why don't you two go for a drink on your own?" she said. We agreed and she pointed us to the local pub. We went into the best room, which was dimly lit and rather empty. There was a stilled silence as we walked in. Ray went to the bar and ordered the drinks for him and me. The barman was talking to him before and after he got the drinks. He came back to me and handed me a glass of cider. "Drink up quickly," he said, "we've got to go."

"Why?" I asked.

"Saturday nights is men only," he said. The barman had told him that he would let me have a drink, but only one, then I would have to leave. That's why they all went quiet when we walked in.

Back home once again we laughed at our second big mistake that evening. We sat for a while and talked to Auntie Mary. She showed us a photo of all six of us as children which I had never seen. We looked a very dirty and sad bunch. Auntie Mary told us

A Saint I Ain't

that she had this photo done one time when she came to stay with us in Yorkshire, and that this was the only copy. I don't think mum ever bought any school photos of any of us, so I had not seen myself as a child. We had photos of ourselves later on after the divorce, but none before I was eleven. We talked until late. Then as we went to go to bed she said in a very serious tone that she was proud of the way I had turned out in spite of my childhood. We hugged each other and I wanted to cry. I fell straight to sleep that night.

The next morning we awoke to the smell of bacon and eggs. It was Sunday morning and Auntie Mary was ready for church. We all had breakfast together, then she went out. We went for a walk down to the loch. It was a beautiful morning. When we got back she was home from church, waiting for us. She said she would like a word with me alone, she had something to tell me. She looked seriously at me and said, "Your father has got TB. He is in a sanitarium near Perth". She told me that she visited him every Sunday after church. She said she was telling me this so that I could decide if I wanted to see him or not. She would go as usual and she wouldn't tell him I was here if I didn't want to see him. He would never know that we had stayed with her and she wouldn't think badly of me if I didn't want to see him. I asked if he was dying and she said yes, the years of drinking and living rough had made him very ill and weak. He was unable to care for himself. She had tried to stop him drinking but without success. He had lived with her after he came up from Yorkshire but the drink had got a grip then, and eventually he left. He came back to her in the late stages of incurable TB. At the moment he was stable, but it was only a matter of time, months or years, no one knew exactly.

I told Ray what she had told me and asked him what he thought. My father had rarely been mentioned over the last year or so. All that Ray knew was that he was an alcoholic and used to fight with my mum when he was drunk. I never told him in any detail anything about our past life. There was no need. He knew all he needed to know about me and he loved me.

We decided that we would go with Auntie Mary to see him.

We thought that if I missed this opportunity to see him, I might regret it if he died. I was also worried about what Auntie Mary would think of me if I didn't go. She had stood by my mum and us, even though he was her brother. Then she had cared for him after we had split up. She had kept contact with us all these years when she had no obligation to. My mother's own family, whom I had never met, had not wanted to know their own daughter and sister knowing full well as they must have, that her marriage would have been a troubled one and children, who were after all their grandchildren, would be suffering in some way. I felt it was my duty to go with my Aunt now and see the brother she still loved and supported when he needed her most. I knew that if I had said I didn't want to see him that she would fully accept my decision and I could have told her no. I also think that a part of me was intrigued as to what he looked like now and how I would feel when I saw him again.

As we drove to the hospital I was glad she hadn't told me the night before. Auntie Mary was a clever lady. She must have been dying to tell me but she knew that if she had told me any earlier than she did I would either have had a sleepless night, or I would chicken out at the last minute. As it was I had little time to think about what we might say to each other, my father and me.

The sanatorium was a hospital especially designed and beautifully landscaped so that the patients could benefit from walking in the gardens to get the fresh air which is important for the sufferers of lung diseases to aid their recovery. It was a very hot and sunny day in early August and all the flowers were in full bloom and the lawns were green and fresh. There were sounds of birds singing all around us giving an added sense of peace and tranquillity to an already calm and peaceful place.

Just as I was beginning to think that this was not such a good idea after all, Auntie Mary reappeared from inside the ward. "I've told him you are here," she said.

Well, that's it I thought, I can't back out now. "What did he say?" I asked. She told me that he was surprised at my unexpected visit. Ray asked me if I wanted to be alone with him but I said no. I wanted Ray to stay with me not only for comfort and reassurance for me, but because I remembered how afraid of him my mother had always been. She lived in fear of him coming and beating her up as he used to do when we were at home. I too felt vulnerable and afraid at this precise moment.

Auntie Mary went into the gardens for a walk and said she would come back in about half an hour. Ray and I went into the ward. I looked down towards the end of the ward. Each bed was allotted its own private space with a little single wardrobe unit and a bedside cabinet. There were screens around some of the beds to give privacy to relatives. It was all very nice and clean-looking and without the familiar hospital smell which I associated with the hospitals I had been in. This had more like a nursing home feel to it. There were flowers on some of the lockers, but most had photos and little ornaments and such on them.

Then I saw him, standing nervously at the side of his bed. As we approached he held out his hand to greet me with a handshake. I introduced him to Ray. He smiled and shook his hand. He looked very weak and sickly. He was much smaller than I remembered. Of course, I was just eleven the last time I saw him so I was a little girl. Even so, he was not the tall erect man that I remembered who fell into the house in a drunken stupor and of whom we rightly were afraid. His strength to beat his wife and sons, and to overpower his little daughter had now been sapped. He sat on the bed and we sat in the two easy chairs put out for us. It took a few moments for the atmosphere to get a little lighter, then he asked how we all were. I had brought the wedding photos for him to see. He was visibly moved as he looked at the pictures. He commented on how well my mother looked, and how the younger children Philip and Jill had grown. They were only about four and five when he last saw them. I wondered if he remembered the day in the courtroom too. The little ones had cried and clung to me. Paul was rude to him and I was very cold towards him. Living with him instead of my mother would never have worked. He wasn't a father, he was a drunken bully.

I watched him now as he displayed real emotion. He

commented something about being sorry that he had missed their growing up, and of course, my wedding. He was still thumbing through the photos as I stared at him. Welling up inside me was not the sympathy which this pathetic sick old man warranted. No. The feelings I had were of bitterness and anger. I resented him ruining our lives with his selfishness. I had no love for him, and unknown to everyone, very little love for my mother too. I felt sorry for my brothers and sister, but love was not what I felt at this moment for anyone. I felt the colour rising in my cheeks as I watched him wipe the trickle of tears from his cheeks. I too wanted to cry, but not for him, for me. I wished I had not said yes to seeing him. I looked at Ray and realised that he could not have known why I was so bitter so I let it all go silently. I was sorry that I could not find compassion in my heart for this man, but he was as much a stranger to me as he was to Ray. I would never see him as a father.

As we got ready to leave he took Ray by the hand and said, "Do ya drink laddy?"

"Not regularly, I like a drink but we don't have much," Ray replied.

"Good," my father said, "look what it does to ya, it ruins your health, and," he looked at me, "I've lost my family because of it."

Now I did feel sorry for him. Tears welled for a second, then I stopped them. I wouldn't give him the satisfaction of seeing me cry. He saw us to the door then, without a hug or anything, which is what I wanted. We walked to the car where Auntie Mary was waiting for us. I looked through the rear window and saw him watch us go. I would never see him again but that was right. I didn't want to.

We were quiet for most of the way home. I was glad I had been now. I would never need to be afraid of him again and I knew that he was sorry. Nothing would make my childhood memories any easier, but at least the main culprit was sorry.

Chapter 8

We packed the car up and prepared to return to our home in Yorkshire on Tuesday morning, the boot filled with wedding presents. Ray's first visit to Scotland would hold many happy memories. We didn't talk about my father again. We had promised Auntie Mary that we would come back soon and next time we would come when the Edinburgh Tattoo was on. Ray would love that. I had seen it once when I stayed as a child. Now I wanted Ray to see it.

Back in Yorkshire we were glad to see our little house. I came to realise that Yorkshire was my real homeland. Scotland was a place of short holidays only. It would always hold memories for me, but the things which were important to me were here in Yorkshire.

Soon we were settled into a pattern of married life. Ray travelled every day to work at the nearby colliery where he had worked since leaving school. I stayed at home and was a proper little housewife. I soon learned to cook and wash and sew as well as looking after the dog. We were very happy. It turned out that Sarah, from my nursing days, and Roger the policeman she had married, were living just a few streets away from us. They now had a baby son. I used to visit Sarah and the baby when Ray and Roger were at work. We relived the happy and fun memories of our Pre-Nursing days and I enjoyed watching her look after the baby. Roger sometimes came to our house while he was working. He was on the beat and would call for a quick cup of tea, usually very late at night, while he was walking his beat. Ray and Roger became very good friends, so much so that Roger talked Ray into applying to join the police force. Both Ray and I thought it would be better than working down the pit for the rest of his life. One night, when he was working, there was a roof cave in at the pit. Although he was not hurt, the thought of what might have been, scared us both. I wanted him out of the pit as much as he wanted to get out. He filled all the forms in and sat a written exam and had a medical. He passed them all and was invited to go to Hendon Police Training College for an eight week selection period some months later. He accepted and we were both very pleased at the prospect of him as a policeman.

As weeks turned to months, we were extremely happy together. We never quarrelled and loved being together all the time. We planned our first Christmas together. Patch had settled in with us too. He was a well-trained, very intelligent dog. He was a good house dog and great company for me when Ray was at work. One day Patch didn't come when I called him in. I looked all around the garden but he was nowhere to be seen. I went out into the street calling him but to no avail. Patch had gone missing for the first time ever. When Ray came in from work I greeted him with the news that Patch had run away. Ray got in the car and searched all over for him. Eventually we went to see Roger at the Police station. It had now been five or six hours since he had gone out. We thought the worst. He must have had an accident. We decided that we must go and tell Ray's mum that we had lost Patch. We drove to her house. By now we were both very upset and we knew that mum would be as well. She loved him as much as we did. We went into the house to tell mum the bad news. When we opened the front door we were greeted by an extremely excited Patch, jumping up and licking us both. Mum said that he had turned up an hour or so earlier on the doorstep. She thought that we had brought him in the car, then she realised that he was on his own. As we were not on the phone she was waiting for Ray's brother or his sister who both had cars, and she was going to get them to bring him back to us. She knew we would be worried. We never knew how he managed to find his way home, which was over five miles from where we lived. Patch did this "home run" three or four times over the next year. We thought that he felt he had to see how Ray's mum was. It was strange how he could find his way, sometimes even in the dark. I said he was intelligent, didn't I?

As we settled down and were approaching October, I began to feel ill. I started to be sick for no apparent reason. After a short while I went to see my GP. He suggested that I had a pregnancy test. I could hardly believe it when the test was positive. I was going to have a baby. This was a total shock to both of us, although we were both delighted at the news. We had never taken precautions to guard against pregnancy but on the other hand we, perhaps naively, didn't think I would get pregnant so soon after we were married. It sounds silly now but we were both pleased and surprised.

When I told Sarah, she was over the moon and gave me lots of tips about what I should and shouldn't do to have a healthy baby. Ray's mum was used to grandchildren and she was very pleased for us. I felt rather embarrassed telling my mother. Ray said not to worry, but, even though I was married, I wasn't sure what she would think of my getting pregnant. When we told her she was as happy as she could be. This would be her first grandchild. I needn't have worried, like Ray had said.

The sickness got much worse and soon I became dehydrated. I was sick all day and all night. My GP had me admitted to hospital. I was about three months pregnant now and we knew that I had never had a period since the week before our wedding. Our baby must have been conceived on our honeymoon. Then we also remembered with concern that we had visited my father who has TB while I must have been pregnant. I told the doctor and he said that they would keep a note of this.

After a couple of weeks in hospital on a saline drip, then a little solid food, the sickness eased and I went home. Within a week it was back and the sickness all day and all night led once more to me in hospital on a drip. This pattern continued throughout my pregnancy. The baby continued to grow and I got larger and larger. I was worried that it would be damaged by my continual illness but the doctors told me that the baby would not suffer. It would continue to get its nourishment from me and grow, and I would have to try to keep some food down for me to stay healthy. I spent about two thirds of the nine months in hospital. This was upsetting for both me and Ray. We were missing each other tremendously.

During this time unknown to me, Ray had heard from the Police Training school and should have done his eight week assessment period. However, he had written to them and told them that he couldn't go as I was ill in hospital. They never sent for him again. I was upset for him when I realised that he had given it up for me. I wanted him to join the police force to get him out of the pit. He said he could not bear to leave me at this time.

About a month before the baby was due we heard that we could have a pit house on the estate near his work. It was also very close to his mum. This was good news. We went to see the house. It was three-bedroomed and had a coal fire, a lovely large garden and the luxury of a bathroom. We accepted it right away. We moved in, with the help of my sister-in-law who helped with the cleaning and the decorating which it needed. I now had just two weeks to go before the baby was due. The nine months had gone much quicker than I had imagined. Maybe it was because of the sickness which has the long medical term of hyperemisis (excessive vomiting), but all the way through pregnancy I never felt maternal. I did the usual things like buying baby clothes and I felt the usual thrills at the baby kicking. Ray said that I bloomed and looked lovely while I was pregnant but I only felt overbalanced and frumpish. I was extremely large towards the end, so much so that I couldn't see my toes and I had difficulty lying down. Then when I did, I couldn't get up again. I never felt good or beautiful, just fat and pregnant. I couldn't wait to have the baby if only so that I could feel normal again.

So when the magic date of April 22nd, the date of my expected delivery came, I was disappointed, as nothing happened. That night

A Saint I Ain't

there was a very funny comedy group on at the working men's club. I wanted to go but Ray was worried in case I started during the evening. As usual I got my way and we went to see the group. They were hilarious and I laughed all night. The rest of our party spent all night telling me to stop getting excited in case I started myself off with laughing. Well I didn't go into labour and we all enjoyed a good night out. That was Easter Sunday.

On Thursday 26th April I started in labour. I have to say that the women who say that giving birth is a "wonderful experience" must know something I don't. I had ten hours of hell, which seemed like ten days. To pot with all this "natural birth" stuff! Give me gas and air any time, and as much of it as I can have without knocking myself out and being no use to the nurses. Eventually when I was so exhausted with pushing that I was falling asleep, the nurse sent for a doctor who delivered my baby with forceps. Then yes, the most uplifting and exhilarating moment did come. As I heard, then saw my baby daughter, it was all worth it and at that moment I would have done it all over again. The nurse put this perfect little human being into my arms and I just cried. She was beautiful. She was 8lb 13 oz at birth. No wonder I looked so big. She obviously hadn't suffered malnutrition while she was inside me. She had the thickest head of jet black hair, so much that even the doctor and nurse commented that it was unusually long hair for a new born baby.

Then it was back to reality. I had two regrets at that moment. One was that I had wanted to have that baby at home and couldn't because I am rhesus negative. The second was that I wanted Ray to be at the birth. In those times husbands were not allowed to be present. As it happens that was probably a blessing for him as, if he had been around about an hour earlier when I was in the full agony of labour, I might have not have been very charitable to him. I would have liked him to see the birth of our child and to be with me when I first held her, as much as he wanted it. He had been sitting just outside the delivery room all the time. This must have been agony for him. As soon as I was stitched, Ray came in. As he saw her he smiled and said, "That's one wedding I've got to pay for." Yuk! How romantic. Nothing like in the telly when you get drowned in red roses and chocolates. Bang goes the violins, this is the real world. We both were over the moon at her and we agreed that she looked the double of her grandmother, Ray's mum. We called her Marie.

Now, at the age of twenty, I was a mother as well as a wife. The first year of my marriage was one of the most special times in my life. Taking out the rough time I had carrying my first baby, the days, weeks and months that followed were a time when Ray and I grew more and more in love with one another. Having Marie made our time together even more happy. I was so proud to be a mum as I'm sure most new mums are.

It gave me great pleasure and personal satisfaction to do all the supposedly boring things associated with being a young wife and mother. It was a time when once again I had to pull out all my resources and effectively cover up my insecurity as a mother, as well as keep quiet about the feeling of disappointment at the way my own mother had left me ill-equipped emotionally as both a wife and a parent. All I had seen in my mother was the bitterness and disappointment in her own marriage. Even when she knew that I was serious about marrying Ray, still she never really showed me and support and guidance which I needed. This support was given by Ray's mum and also his family who did help and direct us and show us both the things we should be doing.

In the first few months of married life, I showed signs of difficulty in our more intimate moments together. Ray was very patient with me, especially at times when, almost beyond my control, I was unable to let him touch or caress me. We never really spoke about this. The time we spent together more than made up for this at the time. In the evenings we played cards or scrabble. When Marie was born, Ray was much more confident bathing and feeding her than I was. After a week or two I got more relaxed about this and I did much more. He was used to small babies, I wasn't. I loved her dearly but I was afraid of her. She was so small and vulnerable.

A Saint I Ain't

As time went on I resented the attention that my mother gave to her. I didn't mind Ray's mum seeing her and we would visit her so that she could see the baby. But when my mother came bringing little gifts I wanted to throw them at her. I didn't let on to Ray though. He thought that me and my mum got on well enough. Little did he know what secrets I was holding.

My character was, and still is such that, all things new and challenging hold a fascination for me. My inquisitive mind remains today, almost childlike in nature. There is a saying which I use often which goes "Little things please little minds". Well, I'm not belittling myself when I say that this saying was made just for me. I am pleased at the simplest of things. I believe that this is because all the simple things in life which are taken for granted were lacking in my childhood. What I did have, I gained all on my own and I had to work twice as hard as anyone else for it. Love was one of the things which had been lacking in my life. The little care I had from my parents was not given out of love, but because they had to do it. Comparing my mother's love with the countless mothers I had met, I saw the shortfall.

Most people take food and family meals for granted. Dinner, breakfast and supper are family gathering times. Laughter and gossip shared over a meal. Learning the all important social skills is done around the family table. Being involved in the preparation of the meal and, yes, even the washing up, all play a part in care for one another. All this was missing, as was the food, in our house. As young children, we fought for the scraps found under the table. Not only emotional, but physical aspects of love and care were lacking.

Our father worked long and hard down the pit and earned good money, but not to feed and clothe his family, to feed his own addiction. When that money was gone he would sell the precious commodity of coal, which was vital in winter, so that he had enough for drink. I don't doubt for a moment that our mother tried to keep us warm but inevitably we went to school cold, and on empty stomachs, then we came home at night to no fire and just enough food to keep us going. Then not enough bedding to keep us warm in bed.

I had gleaned enough from what I saw around me throughout my younger days and into my teens to see what was missing. Their loveless marriage bred unloved children. We were borne out of drunkenness and lust, with feelings of resentment. Conceived as an act of submission, love had no part to play.

When I was young I didn't feel resentful of others, but I told myself that one day I would have these missing luxuries which I didn't get from my parents, both physical and emotional. I was denied love from every angle. Family love was not there. As a child I had few friends. My only love, Andrew, was denied me. I found out after I was married to Ray, from someone who knew me at the time, that it was not Andrew who didn't want to see me, but his mother who had stopped him seeing me when she realised that we were planning marriage. He was from a strict Roman Catholic family. I was "from a bad family". They were protecting their son. True in part, but hardly my fault.

Despite the lack of care, from somewhere inside me grew the instinctive urge to care for others. Could this have come from God, I ask myself? Is this why I became so popular at church? Did people discern the work of the Holy Spirit in me? I don't know. Wherever it came from, I loved everyone so they in turn loved me. My job as a nanny, then as a nurse had both aroused the caring instinct in me. Now I was married and for once in my life I was learning to be loved. Ray loved me for myself. When I was with him, I felt complete. Our love was equal, this was something quite new to me.

When Marie was a year old, I found out that we were to have another baby. On Friday 13th June 1975 I gave birth to Luke. This time I had not had the sickness in pregnancy that I had with Marie. His birth, still without the presence of Ray, was much easier. He, like his sister, was not a small baby weighing 8lb 8oz at his birth. He had ginger hair and looked much more like me than like his dad. I would find looking after my second baby much easier than with my first. My experience of Marie as a baby had taught me a lot. There were not so many firsts for me now. Ray and I were even more in love. I had overcome many of my inhibitions. Some of the things which I thought were forbidden I now knew were OK. Some of the characteristics which I had inherited from my upbringing were being overcome. In Ray and his family I saw love being given and taken. I saw free and spontaneous actions which I wanted for myself. I learned to give them too, but more importantly to take these from my children. As they grew up to walk and to talk and eventually as brother and sister, to interact naturally, my eyes were being opened in such a way as I could never have known without the love I was being given by Ray.

During these two years I drifted further away from my family. Even when I became ill and had to have my appendix removed, it was Ray's family who helped with the children so that Ray could go to work, and his mum who babysat so that he could visit me in hospital. I had only seen Robert and David a few times since my marriage. Paul had remained in the army and never came home on leave. He had met his wife-to-be and spent all his leave with her and her family.

Jill and Philip had left school and they and my mother had stopped visiting us and were all now spending most of their time in bed. What a sad life. I was now finding life and they were losing touch with reality.

I had all I needed in my life in Ray and our children. Every day was new and exciting for me. Ray and I had visited Auntie Mary again after Marie was born. She had stayed with us for two weeks when we had Luke. She went to see my mum and she agreed with me that their way of life had indeed become narrowed and eccentric. We never discussed my father with her.

When Marie was three, she began to go to the local nursery school. Until then, like most young mums, most of my daily life revolved quite happily around my home and family. Taking her to school each day I met other mums and one especially who was to remain a friend forever. Her name was Susan. She had a daughter, also named Marie. Both the girls became friends. Susan and I spent a lot of time together and Luke, who was now eighteen months old, thought that all girls were called Marie as the two girls that he most associated with had, by coincidence, the same name. So every girl he saw he called Marie. Susan went to the local church and she tried her best to get me to go. I still said my prayers and read my bible, although not as much as previously. The children and the house were a full-time job and I often fell asleep as soon as my head hit the pillow. I was not interested in going to church at that time.

Then all the children in nursery and in fact all the infant school, were invited to a children's mission being run by Susan's church. Marie was four by then and Luke two. I did think that I wanted the children to be taught about Jesus as I had been, but I had intended this later on in their lives. As the word went round, most of the children from school were going to this event. So I went along with Marie and Luke in his pushchair. It was a week-long event, meeting each teatime for an hour or so. The theme was George and the Dragon. It was designed for young children whose parents would have to come along with them to join in the stories and games and then to find biblical clues for the children, at home, and take them back the next day for the next clue. At the end of the week was a dragon party, then prizes for all those who had completed the week. Marie loved going to church. She wanted to go every Sunday now.

I soon realised that I was being drawn back to church attendance through the children. They had won where Susan failed. In the end, God got all of us as a family.

As Marie and Luke grew up I was able to recapture even more of my lost youth in the children. Marie started school when she was five, and Luke who was three, began nursery school. I was soon enlisted as a helper in the nursery and I found this rewarding. I also helped out in Marie's class listening to the readers. When mums were asked to go on day trips with the school, I was always the first to offer. Now Christmas had more meaning to me than New Year. It was a time when we all gave one another presents. The children gave us home made cards and gifts and we bought them stockings full of presents. I loved Christmas. Ray played the school Santa at Christmas during the years when Luke was in nursery.

Ray was a wonderful husband and father. He made sure that we had at least one, and often two, holidays a year at the seaside. We would use his sister's caravan. We took the kids' bikes and we all loved every moment. One of my favourite days was bonfire night. Ray built a massive bonfire every year in our garden and we had the loudest fireworks we could find. The children and I made toffee apples and bonfire toffee. Then we made lanterns out of turnips and a big Guy Fawkes to burn. The summer holidays were a special time for me too. The kids and I were never in the house. We spent hours in the park or went for days out. If it was wet, the housework was left and we all baked or made collages or did things, which left the house, the kids and me in a sticky mess. Susan and Marie usually joined in the fun. Little did any one know how much I was getting out of this fun. I never had the chance to play like this when I was young, so I was playing now.

There were sad times for me though when sometimes after a fun-filled day when the kids were in bed and Ray was at work, I would suddenly, without warning, remember the filth and violence of my childhood. I would get both sad and angry at the same time. Then I would creep into the bedroom and see my sleeping children all clean and warm and loved and my tears went away.

These times were very few though and I was usually a very stable and happy mum. I had now become a member of the local Anglican Church and in time Ray started to go as well. We both started confirmation classes. Before I could be confirmed I would have to tell the Priest that I had not been baptised. I put it off because I was afraid to tell him. When I did eventually let my secret slip, he was overjoyed. He would prepare and baptise his very first adult. I hadn't realised the significance of this for a priest. Big plans were in place for me to be baptised. My baptism took place on Easter Saturday night in 1979 during the Easter Vigil. I was confirmed two weeks later in St Mary's Church where Ray and I had been married.

Towards the end of 1979 I realised that we were to have another baby. We had thought about another for a while and now was as good a time as any. This would be our last baby. She was due on Marie's birthday but our second daughter Claire came two days earlier on the 24th April 1980. This time Ray was there at the birth. Now husbands were encouraged to be present. It was perfect. She was delivered and put straight into his arms. She was 8lb 1oz and had black hair, like her sister Marie had when she was born. Ray's presence at the birth was a special moment. He went home after he saw us both settled to tell Marie and Luke the good news. When he told them he didn't get the reaction that he had expected. Marie, who was seven now, let out a loud cry of grief and shouted, "I wanted it on my birthday." Luke, who was five, was also not satisfied. "I wanted a boy," he cried. Then they both rushed upstairs crying, much to the amusement of Ray and our friend. They soon came round though and when they saw her at visiting time that evening they loved her straight away.

"Can she walk?" asked Luke.

"Don't be silly," replied his older and wiser sister, with a gentle punch to his side.

All three of them had to be given a TB test soon after birth because on my father's illness. They were all clear, but the test was repeated annually until they all were five. Best to be on the safe side. Ray and I were now in the eighth year of our marriage.

Chapter 9

Until then we had not had anything traumatic in our married life. As a couple we were very strong and happy. We never argued or quarrelled. We seemed to complement each other in all aspects of married life. We had now completed our family. We had three healthy children. Ray and I had an active part to play in church. Everything was looking good for us. Soon this was to change with long years of medical problems for each one of us. How would our marriage cope with such a strain? Illness can have a devastating effect on a family. I had very rarely been ill in my life. Apart from the problems with my foot when I was in my teens (which turned out to be a benign tumour which was surgically removed), there was a grumbling appendix which had to be taken out when Marie and Luke were toddlers.

But now I was to begin many years of personal illness. It began one evening when Claire was just a week old. During the last few weeks of carrying her, I had suffered with a pain in my chest which was put down to part of the pregnancy. This increased the day I had her and in fact I had become unconscious twice the day they sent me home. One evening while I was bathing her I felt I sharp pain in my chest. I told Ray who grabbed the baby and I lay down on the settee. When the pain got even worse, Ray called for our GP. I don't remember much about what happened next. Suddenly I was lying there, and it was as if Ray thought I was unconscious. I could see and hear everything around me. Marie and Luke were crying and I could hear the baby in her pram against the back wall. Ray was talking to two ambulance men. I was really calm and, although I couldn't move at all or speak, it was as if I thought that those around me could hear my thoughts. I wasn't afraid and I was relaxed. I could still hear everything, but I was speaking to God. I said, "Thank you God for Ray and my kids, I have been very happy."

Then one of the ambulance men put an oxygen mask over my mouth and I came back. The pain came back in my chest and I was taken to hospital. I don't remember anything else until I heard a doctor on the ward saying to the ward sister, "She will need to be in a side ward, I want the baby sent for."

The next day I was told that I had a pulmonary embolism, a blood clot on my lung. They thought that I probably started with it the week I had Claire. She was now in hospital with me. This was the talk of the ward for a while. A new born baby on a medical ward. The nurses would take turns as to who would bath her and feed her. I was in for three weeks and, after a course of Warfarin I went home.

Within a few months I was back in hospital again. This time it was even more serious. I had a severe angina attack. I was rushed to coronary care and kept there for a week. This time I was on medication to prevent a heart attack. It took much longer than I imagined to get back to full strength. Everyone rallied around to help in any way they could. Susan took Marie and Luke to school each day and had them during the weekends and holidays. Our good friend Linda, who lived next door but one, was also a great help in all sorts of ways. Another friend from church called Jenny took care of Claire who was just a few months old. Our GP was very good. He arranged for us to have a home help every day. I never knew that young families had home helps, I thought only old people had them. She came each morning and did the ironing, some of the heavier housework such as the windows, cleaning the paint work, and hoovering and stripping and re-making the beds. The main family washing was all labelled and sent every Monday to a council launderette. It came back on the Wednesday. She did the small daily washing of Claire's nappies and the kids' socks and undies.

A Saint I Ain't

Altogether the support we had as a family, which included extra care from school and the church, held things together to allow Ray to continue to go to work each day and we were all cared for as we needed. We were very grateful to everyone. Without this I don't know how we would have coped. Ray needed to work and the children were young, healthy and active, and I needed to rest to get better. So, after about six months of this routine things were looking much better for us all. No one suffered. Claire thrived, Marie and Luke got all the attention they needed, Ray stayed in work and I got well again. Less than a year after she came to us, the home help stopped coming. She kept in close contact with us for years. Her daughter taught Marie to play the organ.

It had been hard for me to cope with allowing others to play such a large part in my role of wife and mother. These skills had not come easily to me and watching others do them was difficult for me. I knew that as soon as I was well again, all these helpers would leave us and that it was all helping at the time, but I hated letting my small baby go each day to be fed and cared for by someone else. I missed the fun and play times which someone else was having with my older children. I even missed the housework which I enjoyed doing while Ray was at work and the children were at school. Ray and I had as much time as we could together so we didn't drift apart. Luckily, Claire was a really placid baby. She slept a great deal of her first year and when she was awake, she was happy and cheerful all the time. Marie was very bright and well behaved. She was now playing the organ well and had joined the Brownies. Luke, like his sister Claire, was a fairly placid boy. He too was quick to learn at school and was well-liked and popular. Soon he would join the cubs.

My angina never went away completely and I was to have two more stays in coronary care. X-Rays also detected that I had a hiatus hernia which they said I would have had from one of my pregnancies. This, the doctors thought, may be the cause of some of the pain but my ECG tests showed abnormalities as well.

I saw little of my mother and my family during these years.

Ray's mum was old by this time and was often ill and his brothers and sister had all their time taken up with their own families and with their mother. I did see all of them though and regularly. They remained close to us.

In late 1982 another serious illness hit the family. I was now back to full health again and looking after the house and family. One afternoon I was doing the washing when a stranger pushed open my front door and there, over his shoulder was an unconscious Ray being carried by this man.

He put him on the settee, then explained that he had found him lying unconscious near the allotments. He had looked in his pocket and found his driving licence with his name and address on, so he brought him home in his own car. I called our GP who came within half an hour. He said that Ray had probably had a stroke and he would have to go to hospital. He sent for an ambulance. I arranged for Susan to take Claire, and for her to pick Marie and Luke up from school. Then, as I didn't drive, I rang our parish priest who came straight down and drove me to the hospital. There it was confirmed that Ray had suffered a stroke. After some weeks, he was transferred to another hospital for the operation he needed to remove a blood clot from the base of his brain. After this he slowly regained the use of his left arm and leg and it took two years for him to make a full recovery and to get back to work.

During this time, Luke, who was now seven, had a severe fit. This was to be the start of epilepsy. He went to the children's hospital for treatment. Tests proved that he did not have a brain tumour which was the worry that we had. No one knows why some people have convulsions which occur without a fever. Fever is the most common cause of convulsions, but they are not at all harmful to the sufferer. They have no connection at all with mental instability which some ignorant folk fear. With medication, Luke had no problems as a child. We did not treat his epilepsy as an illness and he was not spoiled or sheltered in any way. We would all have to live with this, not just him, so we coped well as a family. We spent hours with him at the children's hospital out-patients. He had regular blood tests, X-Rays and EEG tests. We never seemed to be away from the place.

My angina was finally under control and Ray was back to full strength, Luke was coping with his medication and had just a few minor fits and Claire was nearly old enough for nursery. Then Marie became ill. She had suffered from tonsillitis since she was about two years old. She was on the list to have them removed. The bouts of throat infections were affecting her time at school. She was nearly ten by then and getting ready for going to the secondary school in a year's time. Every four weeks or so she would be ill with tonsillitis. She was on penicillin all the time, which was doing no good at all. Just before Christmas she became very ill. This was worse that I had ever seen her before so I sent for our doctor. When he saw her and examined her said that she must go into hospital right away. He sent for an ambulance to take her to hospital. When it came I went into the ambulance with Marie, while Ray followed in the car. We were told by the doctor at the hospital that she had rheumatic fever, caused by the constant throat infections. The symptoms were severe joint pains and fevers. She was very ill indeed. Marie hated this hospital. As soon as she was well enough, she was moved to the children's Hospital where her tonsils were removed.

After months of treatment she was home and ready to go to the Secondary school. But only now were we told that the joint pains were in fact arthritis. She had repeated bouts of pain and fever for years, and had long spells of illness. Ray and I remained strong during these years. The clock striking midnight on New Year's eve, heralding 1985, saw the beginning of our thirteenth year of marriage.

These years had seen events which would have broken the average couple. Serious illness in all our family members, the closing of the pits and Ray's unemployment, his retraining into the steel works. There was another strain on us which few people were aware of. In these years of our marriage, my family were a constant burden to us. Ray was very patient and kind to them all. But things were getting out of hand. They were demanding more and more attention from us. My mother, and my brothers and sister were constantly in trouble of one sort or another. My mother was taking enough pills to bring down an elephant. She was in a semi-permanent drug-induced sleep now and Philip and Jill were left to cope as best they could. Jill left home and eventually returned pregnant. The baby, a lovely little girl named Lucy, was born a year after our son Luke. Philip had serious learning difficulties and he was getting worse as he got older. He needed constant supervision. My mother, in the few hours she was awake, was becoming more and more odd and eccentric. My older brother David wrote to me from South Africa where he and his wife and two young children were living and asked if he could move in with us when he returned to live in England. This was only to be for a few weeks until they found a house in the area for them to live in. Ray agreed happily and they arrived complete with bag and baggage and a massive Alsatian dog. We still had Patch, so this was a bit of a house full. Weeks turned to months and the problems were mounting, mainly due to overcrowding. There were four adults and five lively children plus two dogs. Eventually they got a house of their own and moved out.

For a while Ray and I had the house to ourselves again. We had missed our privacy. Not long after this my sister Jill had a serious quarrel with my mother and she and her little girl found themselves homeless. She turned up one afternoon with her daughter and two large black bags, asking if she could stay with us until she found a place to live. We took her in. This time it meant Luke had to move into Marie's bedroom and Jill and her daughter Lucy shared the small bedroom. Claire slept in our bedroom. I tried to reunite Jill and my mother but she was adamant that there was to be no reconciliation. They stayed long enough to warrant enrolling Lucy in the same school as Marie and Luke. Lucy and my three got along famously, but, as before, Ray and I were allowed little privacy. After about six months, Jill met

A Saint I Ain't

and married a local man. They then got a flat and we had our home to ourselves once again. Luke moved back into his own bedroom again and Claire returned to share the large bedroom with Marie.

As I said earlier, my mother, Philip and Jill had lost all their social skills by living a semi reclusive life. Even when Lucy got to school age, they found it a problem getting up to take her to school. Needless to say, the state of the house was appalling. Ray and I rarely took the children there, it was so damp and dingy. We had a comfortable home and Marie and Luke began to notice that Granny and Uncle Philip and Auntie Jill were odd. They asked why Granny was always in bed. Philip had now developed into a disturbed adolescent. He did some very strange things, which my mother seemed not to notice. Usually I kept my mouth shut and left them to it but one thing did call for action. I noticed that he had lots of books out of the library. I saw a dozen or more in the living room. Mum and Jill didn't read much to my knowledge, they all preferred the television. When I asked him about the books he said that there were more upstairs in his room. He took me up to show me. To my amazement there were dozens of books all over the room. He proudly told me that he had library tickets in the names of every family member he could think of, including me and Ray and our three children. He had ten or fifteen at least. Each ticket allowed him six books for so many weeks. Then he would rotate the tickets and return so many every two or three days, then get six more out. He never read any. I looked at some of the books and found that none of them were overdue. When I asked him what he wanted with them all, he just smirked and said it was just for a laugh. I made him fill Lucy's pram, and bags too, and we went down to the library. I asked to see the person in charge and when it was all explained he said, "We had noticed that our shelves were looking a bit empty." How stupid could they be not to notice Philip coming two or three times a week with all those tickets. As he never let any of them get overdue, they saw the funny side, but I was embarrassed and annoyed. They took all the tickets from him and left just his own.

My mother reluctantly agreed to come to Jill's wedding. They still weren't speaking to each other but this was to be a full ceremony with white dress and all and Lucy was a bridesmaid. The wedding was to be in the church which I attended, and his family was expecting a real wedding celebration, so she had no choice but to come. My mother, being mother and just to be awkward, made no special effort to look nice. Much to all our embarrassment, she turned up in her everyday coat, head scarf and scruffy shoes. Philip wore an ordinary pair of trousers and an unironed shirt with a jacket with sleeves too short and a button missing and, unbelievably, the talk of the reception, he had cut off all his hair and was wearing a jet black wig, back to front. He looked ridiculous. The pair of them looked as though they had stepped out of Steptoe's back yard. Everyone else wore new wedding outfits. We tried to keep them off the photographs but they strayed into one or two of them. If it hadn't been so sad it would have been funny but the groom's mother was fuming. I laugh now, but at the time I was not amused either.

Quite ironically it was on the morning of Jill's wedding, just after I came in from the hairdresser's and began to dress for the wedding, we got the phone call from Auntie Mary to tell us that my father had died. Perhaps it was because of the day, I'm not sure, but I felt no emotion at all and never have to this day. I asked no details and thanked her for telling me, then we all went to the wedding. We told mum later and she shed a few over dramatised tears and that was that. That was around twelve years after Ray and I had seen him in Scotland.

Within weeks of Jill moving out, one of the worst possible things imaginable happened. I developed itchy spots on my ankles legs and arms. They drove me mad during the nights. After trying all sorts of insect bite creams and sprays they were increasing. Finally I went to the doctor's and he gave me some more cream. Still they got worse. Luke had them too. They kept him awake at night. One night when Ray was on nights at work,

A Saint I Ain't

Luke woke me. He was crying because of the itching. I got up to put some cream on him, then I took him into my bed until he fell asleep again. Taking him back to his own bed before Ray came in from work, I put his bedroom light on I turned down the covers to pop him into bed. To my horror, I discovered the cause of our itching. His bed, and mine too, was covered with bed bugs. My sister had brought us more than we had bargained for when she came to stay. I didn't know what to do. When Ray came home in the morning, he found all of us on the settee. I told him in floods of tears what I had found. We rang the environmental health who came at once and confirmed our infestation. They had to fumigate our house. They said it was very common, not to worry, this happened every day. Well not to me it didn't. Because of my memories of life at home, I had never wanted to be dirty again, now I was. I cried for days. I hated my mother. Later that week we went to her house and I sneaked into the bedrooms and found that all the beds had them. On the way home I was physically sick. My lovely precious home and family had been contaminated, filthy. I wanted to burn everything. I was totally over the top, near to breakdown and feeling hysterical. Once again, Ray was wonderfully strong. It was a good job. I thought that he would blame me. It was my family once again that was causing us so much sadness. When would it end? I wished they would all go away and leave us alone.

My other brother Paul who lived in the south would periodically appear in an old motor home with his wife and four children. Ray and I always used to value the times we had in the evenings on our own. Often, at night when the children were bathed and asleep in bed, we would cook supper and settle down to watch the television together. We very rarely went out and we didn't drink much. Ray enjoyed fishing at the weekends and he played an active role in the church and was a server for many years, as was our son Luke. I was still quite happy staying home and caring for the family. I had never worked since I got married. I did for a short time become a Tupperware dealer and did parties for all the family and for all our friends at church. I did a little waitressing too. I learned silver service and served at dinners at a large banqueting hall. We both did a lot for the church. I became the organist and played for around ten years.

I believe that I had experienced more than my fair share of problems throughout my life. I had some sad memories of my childhood and young adolescent years but for the most part I had always been a positive person making the most of every situation that I had found myself in. Because of my experience of sexual, physical and emotional abuse, the damage would naturally show through at certain times in my adult life. But on the whole up to this time I had no problems at all with the abuse side of my past. My love for Ray and his gentle reassurance when things were difficult made me feel more secure than I ever had been in my life. I wanted to marry him almost as soon as I met him. This was in fact my first true relationship with a man. Suddenly we had a date and time and place and there I was, married not much more than eighteen months after we met. I have never once regretted that day. Without it I would never have experienced the true love of a wife and mother. Marriage, I believe, is truly a gift from God. It allows you to be a complete person in your own right. But as with all God's other gifts, it has to be worked at. My marriage began much like many others. We were young lovers, savouring all the excitement of getting to know each other. Marriage was fun and carefree, building a home and preparing to have a family. Ray worked long and hard at the pit and we had most of the things we needed for our physical and material comfort. But as well as all this fun, we were learning more about life than we realised. There is growth in two people getting to know one another. Trust too is important. Love and trust cannot be separated. The actual wedding ceremony, after months of planning, seems to be over in such a short time, and the first years of marriage rush by so fast that young lovers hardly have time to get to know each other. Even more so for us as we had Marie within a year of our wedding day.

Everyone presumes that because you are showing outward

signs of happiness, that you must be truly happy. But in my case, this was not so. No one, including Ray, knew how much I was hurting inside. Sometimes his touching me made me want to scream. I was screaming inside but he didn't know. I had learned to control my feelings, to scream in silence. Nightmares, awake and asleep, haunted me but still I said nothing. It will be OK, I told myself. It will go away, it will pass, but it never did. The problems were not of memories, incidents or the actions of people from my past, it was the feeling of inability to cope with being loved and of loving; of not being able to be touched and caressed, and of finding touching another person very difficult. These things do not come naturally to someone who has never experienced them.

I say no one knew but that's not quite true. God knew. Even then, long before my eventual confirmation years later, as a young wife and new mother, I felt the touch of God's hand in my life. My prayers and bible study kept me in touch with God. It would be a few years until I began to attend a church, joining other Christians to worship and eventually become a full member of His church at the age of twenty-seven. But for now I took comfort in a very private and personal journey with God which had no need of others, or of the sacraments which would become so important to me.

Late in 1983 and early '84 I had begun to show signs of illness again. My periods had become erratic, stopping for months, then coming all the time for weeks on end. The pulmonary embolism and following angina made it obvious that another baby would not be wise. We were happy with three children anyway. Our GP gave me iron tablets and said it would all settle down, but it didn't. Some days I was so weak that I couldn't get up. I had a constant headache and felt sick all the time. I struggled on, often feeling as though I had sand bags on my eye lids, I wanted to sleep all the time. One afternoon when I was walking back home from taking Claire to the nursery, I began to feel faint. It was as though the ground beneath my feet went soft and I was walking right into it. Then, right there on the main road, everything went white and I collapsed. Someone called an ambulance and I was taken to hospital. I was given an immediate blood transfusion and admitted to the ward. The doctor told me that if I hadn't had medical treatment that day, I might have died. My blood count was so low it was off the scale and I needed two more blood transfusions before it was normal. I was so pale that the young and very caring medical student who cared for me, dubbed me Snow White.

"How's Snow White today?" he would ask when he came to see me.

Soon I was much better. The headache went and I wasn't sick and tired any more. It appeared that I had something called endometriosis, which is a condition often associated with having children. Within six months I was back in hospital for a hysterectomy. It seemed that I had spent so much time in hospital over the recent years. I was becoming worried that people would think that I enjoyed the attention or something. But each individual illness was real. When I was admitted, I was very weepy. This was not, as one might think, because of some female yearning to keep my womb, the sooner I got rid if this nuisance the better. I had no after effects emotionally from the operation as it happened. The tears were of frustration. Every time I seemed to be on a good run, one of us was ill. This is very wearing emotionally. Now I was waiting to have a major operation which would take months to recover from, and I wanted to be well right now. I was missing being well. It seemed such a long time since I had really felt well. The angina had remained a constant problem to me and I was now on permanent medication for that.

The day before I went into hospital I had received communion and anointing from my priest. Since my confirmation five years earlier my Christian friends and the clergy had been a big support to me and Ray. As a family we had seen so much illness that without support we could not have managed sometimes. We certainly got that support from church. Our whole life seemed to be ruled by doctor's appointments and hospital visits for one or the other of us. Now even Claire had developed a rare condition called geographical tongue which is thought to be unknown in babies and is usually only seen in adults with false teeth, would you believe. Her tongue developed deep cracks in it. It wasn't painful but looked so bad that at school the nursery teacher asked me to bring her own cup in as they were worried other children would catch it. They were not reassured when I told them that it wasn't contagious. It is a lifelong condition which she will have to live with.

In hospital before the hysterectomy I had a visit from the chaplain who I had come to know very well over my years as an in-patient. We spoke a lot about my love and trust in God which was so important to me. I told him how I was feeling about all our illnesses and he was kind and understanding. While I was in, as had happened so may times before, my faith had become a talking point with other patients as my priests visited me and I had regular visits from the chaplain. Some of the people who were in with me actually came to faith while others who had fallen out with God or the church came back to God. So I may have in fact been used by God to help others in spiritual need while I too was being cared for in a special way by the church in their support during our families illnesses. It sounds as though I am a martyr. Well I'm not. Continual suffering I had, but patience was something I was blessed with at this time in my life, having less and less of it as time went on and more problems came our way. Sometimes over the last few years and now during my recent spiritual struggles, I blamed God for everything; my illnesses, my families illnesses, my extended family problems and my past. If God had called me, as I knew he had, why was he giving me so much grief? I couldn't fault the church. The clergy and people had been tirelessly supportive throughout all our troubled times. But I did blame God at one stage.

Remarkably even during the worst times, Ray and I remained blissfully happy with each other. The bad times were bringing us together, not dividing us. We had no time to row and bicker I suppose, we had to care for each other and together we had to care for the children. We gained strength as a family from our faith too.

I had more problems with bleeding for over a year after my hysterectomy. Eventually after a course of treatment which included cauterising the neck of my womb at the site of the bleeding, the bleeding stopped and everything healed as it should do. During all this treatment and internals, which meant continually being examined by male doctors, I was feeling very insecure. Any woman going through this would feel the same, but for me with the traumatic incidents of my past which were unknown to everyone, every time I was examined I went through hell.

For a year or two life rolled gently by and we saw little of my family. Then in early 1986 my mother, who had now moved into a small flat, began to be ill. She had remained a very heavy smoker and was now smoking about sixty a day. She still slept an unnatural amount of time and her diet was poor or non-existent. She had lost a great deal of weight and was now looking very ill. She was diagnosed as having lung and bone cancer. In May 1986 she was admitted to hospital. I went to see her every day and within two weeks realised that she was dying. She was moved to a single room. Jill and Philip had visited her every day, but now it was time to send for the others who lived away. Paul, David and Robert came during the last week of her life. It was strange how it happened but on the evening of the last day of her life, only I went to the hospital to visit her. It was a Sunday and I went in the afternoon to find her alone and sleeping in her room. Usually either Jill or Philip was there or would come at some time. This day no one else came at all. When she woke up she asked, as she always did, to be helped to the toilet where she could have a cigarette. I tried to help her but she had great difficulty standing. One of the nurses who was near told me that she could go back to her room and have a smoke in bed. It was obvious that she had perhaps only days to live and stopping her smoking now was unrealistic.

We rarely spoke when I visited her other than petty

A Saint I Ain't

conversation and we never spoke about her death. Now I knew that the time was near. She lay on her bed and was in severe pain. Every hour or so a nurse came and gave her pain relief, but the pain was too great for anything to help her. As eight o'clock came near and visiting time was over, the sister came in and saw her sleeping. She told me that if I wanted to stay I could. We both knew that she was going to die soon. I debated when I should call for the others to come. The sister said she would live through the night and I should call them in the morning. I had let Ray know that I was staying all night. I sat with her and every so often she came round from her sleep and asked for medication or to be lifted onto the commode. She was so small that I was able to lift her on my own. Every movement caused her excruciating pain. I was as gentle as I could be but it was hard. While she was sleeping I watched her and my thoughts were very sad. Why had she not cared for us all? Why had she not been a real mother? At this moment I didn't hate her, but I felt no love for her. While she was asleep I touched her arm, trying to give both her and me some comfort, but we were both cold. I felt nothing but sadness. I didn't cry as I thought I would, I just sat there and stared at her. During the night she sometimes opened her eyes and stared back at me but no words were spoken.

As daylight broke, the nurse who had been in and out all night brought me a cup of tea. As I was drinking it my mother said, without moving or opening her eyes, "I'm going to him." Then as I watched, her breathing began to sound bad and I knew that she was slipping into a coma. I walked across to the main building to ring Ray to come and pick me up and I contacted the rest of the family. It was now that I realised that I should have rung them earlier so that they could be with her before she was unconscious. But it was too late now to worry, as it happened they never questioned my actions. Back in my mother's room I thought about her last words. There were two people she could have been referring to. One was my father, the other was God. I thought in the car on the way home of the things she had done in bitterness and I was angry at her for not putting them right when she had the chance to after she and my father split up.

By nine o'clock we were all at my mother's bedside. She was now in a deep coma. Jill was crying hysterically and uncontrollably and Philip was not far off. I fought back the tears and Paul, David and Robert just stood and watched. Within the hour she died.

At her funeral were just her six children and the few grandchildren who were old enough to be there. After a small gathering at my house, everyone went home. Soon my life was going to change, and this time I would never be the same again. The weeks following my mother's death were difficult for me. Although I had little love for her, I had not spoken openly to anyone about this. Not Ray or any other family member knew. The rest of my family had their own grieving to do. I never spoke to my Christian friends or priests about my family. At this time I thought that they would condemn me for not having the right Christian attitude towards my family. Without revealing things from my past which were nobody's business, they could never understand anyway so I kept it all to myself.

Because I had no bitter or resentful feelings towards her, Marie, Luke and Claire loved their Granny. They knew that she was a little strange and they thought Philip was great. They had seen little of them since the argument with Jill but what they did see they had no reason not to like. Our family had never really been close. We had now all gone our separate ways. In 1984, two years before she died, my mother must have been going through some serious crisis in her own life which we were unaware of. She was a nasty bitter lady. Not long after Jill had come to live with us, Philip and my mother had a fall out over something and he too was cast out from his home. This was a sad affair as Philip had never been able to care for himself. He was always slow and could not hold down any kind of work and would not be in any fit state mentally to live alone. He came to me and asked if he could live with us. This was never a possibility. He needed to be cared for. My mother had moved to a single flat and didn't want Philip to know where she was. He had a violent side to his character and had threatened to kill her. She was,

A Saint I Ain't

quite justifiably, afraid of him. He had threatened to set fire to my house when I told him that he couldn't live with us and he pestered us with phone calls and visits during the night and day for a while. He refused all other offers of help to him. He wanted his mother but she didn't want him. My children had to come first, and besides I was not about to take on the problems that Philip would bring with him. It may have been a selfish move, but we stuck it out until soon he stopped coming and disappeared. At first I was worried, then I accepted that there was nothing I could do for him.

Months later I received a letter from a prison chaplain saying that Philip was in prison. Even now he wanted to come to us when he had served his time. After long discussion, Ray and I decided once again that we would not care for him. The risk to ourselves and our children was too great. We replied to the chaplain by letter and never heard from Philip until after he came out of prison and eventually married a Christian lady. I think it was through the prison chaplain that they met, although to be quite honest, this period in my family's life is all a bit cloudy to me.

Jill took my mother's death very badly. My mother had been living with Jill since her wedding. It was Jill who finally got her the medical help she needed, albeit too late. After her death, Jill felt very guilty and went into deep depression. She cried on the phone to me for hours. There was nothing I could do to stop her feeling that she was in some way responsible for her death. Philip too came to see me and rang a lot. There was nothing I could do that would bring his mother back which was all he wanted. Sometimes he went on a drinking binge. During these times it was wise to steer clear of him. Sober, he was known to have a quick temper, but drunk he was frightening. Paul and David were badly affected by our mother's death. They also had times when they drank too heavily. It seemed that all the boys in the family turned to alcohol to blot out the bad times. Robert was drinking more than usual and his wife was worried about him.

Chapter 10

About a month after the funeral we were asleep when, in the middle of the night, we heard a banging on the front door. It was David. He was absolutely blind drunk. I turned on the landing light and started to go downstairs. When I reached the bottom step I heard David crying uncontrollably on the doorstep. He was crying, "Mary, let me in, I want my mother, I want my mother."

That was the precise moment when I had taken all I could take of my family. I dissolved into floods of tears and, not opening the door, I screamed at him, "Go away and leave us alone." I sat on the bottom step and wept bitterly for the first time since the funeral. Ray ran downstairs and hugged me while I cried. Then he opened the door, saw David into the living room and then came back to me. He took me back to bed, then went to see to David. He had fallen into a drunken sleep on the settee.

The next day Ray took him back home and told his wife that I was to be left alone. He rang all the rest of my family and told them the same. They all had to sort themselves out. We had done all we could for them, now we needed privacy. Thank goodness I had Ray. He saved the day once again.

Now the floodgates of my past had opened and the beginning of my breakdown began. I tried not to let things get on top of me, but soon I was seriously depressed. Depression was something that I had never suffered from. This may sound surprising with my background but it is true. Throughout my life even when things were really bad, I covered my feelings with a smile and had never allowed myself to get depressed. This was not always easy, but I usually managed to smile through most things.

About a year before my mother's death when things were going reasonably quietly, I applied and was accepted to be a Samaritan. I found this voluntary work to be just right for me. After a six month probationary period I was a full member of the branch. The listening came easily to me. People had always told me things which they found hard to tell others and confidentiality was very important. Friends knew that if they confided in me, they could be reassured of my silence. I soon realised that the ethos of the Samaritan movement was identical to what I had been doing. One thing which I was good at was not taking on board the troubles of others and letting their problems bother me, and most importantly, not trying to solve their problems, simply letting them talk through the things which they needed to talk about, then letting them find their own solution. At this time I really didn't have any problem with my own past. I continued as a Samaritan with only a very few people knowing that I was one. I therefore knew all the tell tale signs of depression from the work I did as I slipped further and further into it myself. I was unable to stop myself and I didn't ask for help. There were so many things from my past which were suddenly troubling me, all arising from the feeling of being unwanted and unloved as a child. Things from the past like songs on the radio or television, sounds and smells, even people discussing their younger days, all these sent my mind into overdrive. My mother's death had uncovered feelings of bitter resentment of her lack of ability as a mother, and hatred of my now dead father who had abused me. I began to hate myself and I wanted others to hate me too. I wanted to be that dirty child I once was, so that people would treat me like the kids and adults did when I was little. Still I told no one.

At first I was able to continue with my normal household routine. I had most of my bad thoughts at night when the children were in bed and Ray was fast asleep beside me. In the daytime I felt reasonably all right. The most intimate part of our marriage suffered of course. This was the first thing to happen. When Ray touched me I wanted to scream. He was patient with me but it got so bad that I would get up in the early hours of the morning and not go back to bed. I got so tired that I wanted to sleep all day. I began to blame Ray for my sleepless nights.

Then it strayed into the day time. The housework went. The house became a mess and I didn't care. I smoked anyway but my smoking increased tremendously. I was weepy all the time and snapped and argued with Ray over the least little thing. I was never this way with the children but my easy and carefree attitude to them was affected. I couldn't be bothered to interact with them any more and they knew. We used to have such fun together and I loved to read to them and hear them read, but all this gradually went as the weeks turned to months.

Ray was the only one who knew that there was a problem and he never told anyone. At church and in school I always put on a relaxed and happy front. It was at home where I let myself go. I stopped cooking for the family and ate very little. I was rapidly losing weight and eventually I went from my normal nine stone to under seven stone. Still no one seemed to notice. I was so sad inside but I continued to smile as normal. At one stage I tried to tell my parish priest but I didn't know where to start.

I wanted to cry all the time but I couldn't. Whenever I thought about my parents I went more and more back into my past. Sometimes I would resent the things my children had. The books, the toys, the clothes, everything. Earlier in my marriage these were the very things which I had enjoyed, now I hated these objects. My mind was clouded with irrational thoughts. A part of me knew that I was being irrational and yet I couldn't stop myself. I would sit for hours during the day and think about all the bad things which had happened to me. I wanted to tell my parents how much they had hurt me. Now it was their fault that I could not care for my children, as they hadn't cared for me. I blamed my brothers and sister who had slowly driven me into this state. Their inability to cope had rubbed off on me, I thought. They had always said that I was the lucky one. I, they said, was the normal one. "Well," I would tell them bitterly in my mind, "I hope you are satisfied now all of you, I am like you now."

A Saint I Ain't

Then it was all Ray's fault. If he hadn't let my family come and stay with us, if he had stopped my mother from seeing us, if he had got that job in the police force, we might have been living far away and we would never have seen my family.

When he came in from work, I started an argument almost every day. Then I would storm out of the house, satisfied with what I had achieved and escape from the house and him and the kids. I would go to one of my church friends' houses and act as though everything was fine. I could switch these feelings on and off when I was with others, no one would have known that I had just had a blazing row with Ray. I returned when he was in bed. Then I would slide in beside him, turn my back to him and lie awake thinking about everything until daylight. Then I got up and as soon as he moved, I went back to bed and he would have to get the kids up and ready for school. On and on it went, getting worse every day. My self-esteem was nil. Never at any stage did I think of asking for help. It was as if I wanted to be like this. I had been strong all my life I told myself, why should I let go now?

There came a time when I wanted people to know that I was this bad person really, not the nice Mary who loved everyone and whom everyone loved. So my plan was thought out during the long dark hours of the night. While all this was going on in my mind, real life was happening all around me. I was still taking full part in the life of the church, playing the organ on Sunday, helping with the Sunday school. In school too I was helping in the nursery, hearing children read in the infants school, going on school trips with the kids. My friend who got me the waitressing job asked me to help out working two mornings a week at a snack bar. I had been doing this for some time before the depression started. I wanted to stop all these things but I couldn't think of reasons to tell people why I had stopped.

Now I wanted to run away. I wanted to escape from all the bad things which I thought were now happening because I was bad. The thoughts I was having would stop if I left Ray and the kids. I was a bad mother and a bad wife anyway, and they would be much better without me. I thought that if I had some money I could go away. I only had the family allowance and that was spent on dinner money and shopping which I had to pay. In the night I planned that I would go away. I would get a little flat on my own, change my name of course, live at the seaside where I would get a job in a cafe or a hotel as a waitress. Or I would live in as a housekeeper in a big house as I had done when I was a nanny. I could look after the children or be a companion to an old lady who, in return, would let me have the run of the house. No one would know me. I knew that Ray and the kids wouldn't look for me. He would tell everybody that I had gone away to work. Nobody would think it was strange. Lots of people go away to work. But first I needed my train fare. I couldn't ask Ray for it or he would find out that I was going away.

Then began the time of real running away. This was exciting. I would get the kids off to school, then get on the bus to town or to the city. I would walk around all day or go to a park and then usually I went home. But sometimes as people slowly disappeared from the city or town in the evening, I would find a corner to sleep in. A park bench or the public loos were my favourite places. I was moved off by the police sometimes. This was fun, no one knew that I was really a wife and mum running away from the responsibilities of home and family. Then I would return home to another almighty row from Ray.

"Where have you been?" he would ask. I would either ignore him or have a row back, depending how I felt. He must have been so worried, but at the time I didn't think about him or the kids. Or I would wait until he came in from work and the kids were in bed, then I would go round to someone's house and stay till midnight or one o'clock drinking tea with a friend who would be unaware that Ray was worried that I might not come home.

Ray did sometimes ring round our church friends to see where I was. This would send a chain reaction of calls until eventually it became apparent that we had a problem. Then Ray spilled the beans and told of my depression. I was eventually spoken to by my parish priest who, although very sympathetic, simply missed the serious stuff. He must have assumed that Ray and I were having marital problems which was understandable. I didn't correct him, but let him think this because at that stage my mind was in such a state that I was unable to explain what the root cause of the problem was. He said that when I felt like running away I just had to ring him or the curate and it would all be OK. Of course it wasn't as simple as that. It wasn't just a marital problem. I was causing my husband and children severe problems and our marriage was suffering, but it was a personal crisis I was going through. Marriage guidance was not the answer at that time, but I agreed with my priest and Ray that we would go for counselling. I skimmed over the truth and told them about my problem with Ray touching me. They never asked and I never disclosed anything about my past. Still even Ray knew nothing.

The next stage of my downward spiral was lying. I was now lying to Ray about everything. You name it, if he asked me something, I would lie, even if I didn't need to; where I had been that day, who I had seen; ridiculous and unnecessary lies. I would tell him I was going to the shop, then go for a long walk and go home again. I would say I was going to one friend's house, but I would go to another. If there was something on at church I would say I was going, then not go and come home and say I had been. Each night I would lie awake and my head was filled with confusion. I was being tormented by my own thoughts. I wanted to run away.

I went through a weepy period. I would burst into tears at Ray every day. Now I wanted to talk to someone. I plucked up courage and asked to speak to our young curate at church. I would tell him everything, I thought, as I lay in my bed one night. He will make it all better, I thought.

I walked up to church ready to tell him all about my past and why I was acting as I was. I sat at the back of church and through the tears I told him. But in fact a great pack of lies. I said that I was taking drugs. I hadn't meant to lie to him and I hadn't pre-planned this drug story, this came to me as I was sitting with him. I had really meant to tell him but I didn't know where to start. He was very kind and, believing me as he had no reason not to, said that he would get me the help I needed. The symptoms that I was showing must have looked very much to him to be in line with my lie. He and my parish priest now knew that I had been staying out all night, and that Ray was now at his wits end as to why I was like this, so it may well have been true. He asked me many details and I made up this fantastic pack of lies to answer all his questions. He asked if I would see him next week to let him know how I was. I agreed.

As I lay in bed that night I realised that I was digging myself deeper into trouble but still I couldn't face reality. I was very sad and unhappy. After seeing the curate for a few weeks and reassuring him that I was now off the drugs, he said I must tell my parish priest now. I hadn't expected this and it threw me into more confusion. I was getting away with it now and soon, I thought, I could have told him that I was better and he would not see me again. He arranged for me to see the priest. Reluctantly and unable to get out of it, I agreed. This frightened me. I would have to lie to him now and I didn't want to. I was more afraid of this because he was the rector. I spent all that night in bed trying to think of how I could get out of this one. The next day I wrote a long letter to the curate telling him I was very sorry but I had lied to him and that I had never been on drugs. Still I didn't tell him about my past. I pushed this through his letterbox, than went home. He rang me and asked me to see him in church.

I was shaking with nervousness as I waited in church for him. Although I could tell that he was annoyed with me for lying, he was very restrained and we spoke for a long time about my depression. I promised that I wouldn't lie to him again and he released me from my appointment with the rector for which I was very relieved indeed. I didn't want to continue this lie. I felt really embarrassed and sorry every time I saw him. In truth I am not a liar and I hated the thought that he might never trust me again.

Things remained bad at home. Ray and I argued a lot and the lying continued. The leaving home was the same. Later that year

A Saint I Ain't

members of the parish would be going for our annual weekend pilgrimage to The Shrine of Our Lady of Walsingham. I had been on every weekend pilgrimage as long as I had been at this church. Part of the preparation for this weekend was to go to confession. This I did regularly anyway. I had been to confession since this all began and I had confessed everything to our new curate. I had promised God that I would stop but I knew that I couldn't, now I needed help and I knew it. The new curate was not as understanding as the old one and I knew I would be in trouble if he found out that I hadn't arranged to see someone for help. He had warned me that if I didn't do something about it, he would. This firm attitude was not right for me, and it made me more depressed. He heard my confession in Walsingham and was, as I expected, not pleased when I had not made a move to get help. He was very firm with me and said that he would see me back into parish. I was afraid that he might tell the Rector or Ray, although the rules of the confessional forbid him to do this, so I thought he might make me tell them. I planned then and there to run away when we got back home.

Within a week I left home again. I got on my bike this time and actually packed a few clothes. I cycled all the way to where Philip and his wife lived. I arrived in the late afternoon and Philip let me in. They were surprised to see me. I hadn't rung as I had on the few occasions that I had been to see them before. I usually went with Ray in the car so they were surprised when they saw the bike. I liked Pam, Philip's wife. She was a caring lady who was very good to Philip, giving him the love and care he needed. We talked at first about my children, then about hers. Then I told them the lie I had prepared to explain why I had come. I said that Ray and I had split up and I needed somewhere to live. They were stunned into silence. They never thought Ray and I even rowed, let alone would leave one another. They asked if Ray knew where I was and I said no. They wanted me to ring him to let him know that I was safe but I refused. After a long time of talking and a lot of lying, Pam went into the kitchen to make another drink. Then she used the bedroom phone and called Ray. She came through and said that Ray wanted to speak to me. I was angry at this but I agreed to speak to him. He had realised that I had gone because I hadn't picked the children up from school and a friend had to take them home until he came home from work. He had rung round everyone to see where I was. He never imagined that I would go to Philip's. I had not seen any of my family since my mother's funeral almost a year earlier. And Philip was the last one he thought I would go to. I only had the choice of two, Philip or Jill and I could never confide in Jill. David had moved near to Paul now and I didn't want Robert to know that I was having trouble.

Ray asked me to come home and I said no, I needed some time to think. I agreed to ring him again later. I didn't tell him about the curate as I should have done. It would mean telling him everything. Philip went to bed and left Pam and me to talk. I can't remember what I told her, but it was far from the truth. Around nine o'clock I rang Ray to say I would come home the next day. When Ray answered the phone he said he was relieved that I was safe and that he loved me and wanted to see me better. Then he said he had someone with him who wanted to speak to me. To my horror the curate was at my house with Ray and he came on the phone to speak to me. I went to pieces when I heard his voice. He said to come home and we would sort everything out. When Ray came back to the phone I was so angry at him for letting the curate speak to me. Ray was confused but said not to be upset because everyone wanted to help me. I lay awake all night, worried that everyone would know about me. The school would know now. All the church folk would be talking about me. The curate and probably the rector would be waiting to tell me off. Ray would be angry at me, not to mention the poor kids who must now know that something was wrong.

What a mess. How would I get out of all this?

The next day I went home on my bike. Ray was waiting for me and he wasn't annoyed, he was worried. The rector did indeed want to speak to me - not to tell me off, but to try to help both me and Ray.

A Saint I Ain't

Ray and I went to the Rectory together and I cried a lot and got a lot of sympathy. I agreed to see my GP and go on anti-depressants but still I said I didn't know why I was depressed.

As soon as we left the rector's study, I turned on Ray and we argued in the car. How dare he force me to get help when I hadn't got a problem, I screamed at him. I told him I would leave home if he forced me to go to my GP. Poor Ray, it's a wonder he stayed so strong through all this, but he did.

Now I was entering the last and most traumatic phase of my depression. Back home I went to my bedroom and cried. My mind was racing. I wanted to run away but I had nowhere to go. I had to keep up the outward show of getting better so that I kept the rector happy. The curate was leaving soon and I was glad about that. He had in fact upset Ray when he came to our house while I was at Philip's. Ray hadn't invited him but he came when one of our friends told him that I had gone missing again. The truth was, he was partly to blame for that. I couldn't face seeing him, but only he and I knew that. Ray thought that I would come home if the curate spoke to me. He didn't realise what he had done. Then, after he came off the phone to me, the curate had told Ray that he should be harder on me, he was too soft. Ray was angry about this. Although he knew nothing about the abuse I had suffered, he knew that my father was violent and that I had witnessed as well as sampled the violence of both my parents. Being gentle in nature, Ray would never resort to violence and to have a priest suggest such a thing to him was unacceptable. However, out of respect for his position, Ray kept silent. He told me about it many years later.

As weeks went on I began to think that people were talking about me. When I took Claire to school, I thought the parents at school and the teachers were looking at me and talking about me behind my back. I hated going out. Even in church, I was sure the curate, who had now left, had told everybody that I was stealing from church and they were all watching me. Soon I stopped going. Then I thought the people at the post office and the bus stops were talking about me so soon I wouldn't go out. I got Marie and Luke to take Claire to school and when they said that the teachers and parents asked how I was, I knew that they really were talking about me. I thought they were saying I was mad. "Nutty as a fruit cake," I thought they were saying.

I had let the house and myself go a long time ago, but now it was worse. Soon I spent all day sitting in a chair by the fire staring into it and in a world of my own. During the day my mind was a blank. I couldn't do anything, not even answer the door or the phone. I wasn't having panic attacks, I was numb. It was as if I was drugged or drunk. I was in a permanent docile dream all day long. When the children came in from school they got their own tea and got ready for bed themselves. I wasn't angry at Ray anymore when he came in, I just sat in the chair and ignored him.

At night-time my mind woke up. I would go to bed and as soon as Ray was breathing deeply I would turn on to my back, and peering into the half-light of the bedroom, thoughts came to me of the things from my past; incidents which happened and, worst of all, the feelings around them as if it were happening now. I hated my mother most of all, for the things she did and for the things she should have done to protect me from all the bad things people did to me. I hated my father for being an alcoholic and for this being the reason I went into care and had to suffer once again. Night after night different things came back to me. The sounds, the smells, the feelings.

Ray lay sleeping while I endured the terror of the nights. When I did sleep, I dreamed the same things, only now people from the present were in my nightmares. The headmaster from school, the milkman, the lady from the post office, priests, neighbours, bus drivers, they were all out to get me. They knew my parents and they thought they were lovely. They all said that I was making up lies to get my parents into trouble. I was bad and no one liked me.

Awake again and in a cold sweat. I knew that I was dreaming but I still felt as if my heart would burst, it would beat so fast with

A Saint I Ain't

terror. Downstairs at three or four o'clock smoking and drinking tea, I wished it would be morning, then I could sit by the fire and stop thinking all day. During the day I tried hard to bring myself back to the real world, but it was too hard.

In the night I began to experience serious hallucinations even when I was awake. I could clearly hear my neighbours talking about me. I recognised their voices. She would say, "Can you hear her, she's at it again, every night's the same, crying and screaming all night long, it's disgusting. And she's not looking after those kids you know. They're dirty, like the house, she should be ashamed of herself, letting things go like that." Then her husband would agree. My heart would pound with terror as I listened. Then it would go quiet and I would go to the wall and press my ear against it. They were asleep now, and I would have to stay awake so that I didn't make a noise and wake them.

During the day I was afraid to see them. I really believed that this was happening so I expected them to say something to me over the garden fence. In the early evening when the children came home from school and before Ray came in from work around five, I had to try to see to them but it was impossible. If they went into the garden to play, I thought they were telling my neighbours on the other side of us. "Mum can't look after us," I imagined they would say. Then if there was loud laughter from either side of the fence, they were laughing at me. When Ray came in I went up to the bedroom until the children were in bed, then I would sit in the living room with Ray who would try, without success, to hold a conversation with me.

A new curate came to the parish, and whether by accident or the design of the rector, he came to see me one day. I liked him straight away and I found that I could speak to him. I later found out the he too was a Samaritan but at first I had no idea. He listened easily and I soon found myself opening up to him. He arranged for me to see him in his house each week and, without realising what was happening, I began to release some deep feelings to him. He asked me to write down the things I wanted to say and couldn't, then I was to bring them to his house and read them to him. Then we tore them up. Things began to look brighter for a month or two as my feelings were explored. It was never threatening to me and I felt much better. Then he said one day that I should consider professional therapy. He said that he knew a place where I could have further counselling which he was not able to give me. I agreed willingly. But when the leaflets came and he asked me to fill the form in and send it back to get and appointment, things went wrong.

As I read the booklet which accompanied the form, I thought that I didn't in fact need therapy but that I could be a counsellor. I was so pleased because now that the curate had helped me to get better, I imagined that I could help other people in the same state as me. I really believed that the few weeks of talking had cured me. I was of course still very depressed and was nowhere near ready to help others, but I couldn't see this. When I told the curate that I was going to be a counsellor and that I wasn't going to have any therapy, I was truly surprised at his annoyed reaction. What did I do wrong, I asked myself? Why wasn't he pleased for me? He then began to ignore me, making excuses when I tried to arrange to see him. Within a day or two I was back where I was when I first started visiting him. My world fell apart once again. My fragile mind couldn't take his rejection.

Once again sleep eluded me. There was no escape from my irrational and hostile thought patterns. My reason and judgement were seriously impaired. My downward descent had gradually reached its deepest point. I was reaching despair.

Now the night-time horrors waited for me, waited to torture me mentally and physically. My body cried for rest, but there was none to be found, my mind withheld it. In the dark hours of the night and the grey of the dim bedroom, I would lie in a state of half-sleep, as if drunk or drugged, though neither substance had passed my lips for months.

My mind was alive with unpleasant desires, angry and bitter thoughts and memories too painful to feel in the light of day. As I lay there, my head ached with a constant dull pain. My eye lids were heavy through lack of sleep. Sweat gathered and ran around the creases of my neck, arms and legs. My arms felt too long and too thin, my legs felt too heavy as if weighted down with sacks of cold damp sand. My fingers twitched uncontrollably all the time. Sometimes I rubbed my greasy hair between finger and thumb with one hand while the other hand forced itself into my mouth as if to stop the outward rush of breath which wanted to release a loud scream into the room and couldn't.

All the time I was listening to Ray's breathing which was loud and deep. I was angry at him for sleeping while I was going through hell all alone. In the days before the end, Ray became a monster in my mind. As he slept he would move towards me. Unconsciously in his sleep his arm or his leg would touch mine. I would flinch and draw back, screaming loudly and frightening him into waking up. Suddenly I didn't know this person who was lying in my bed beside me. I was afraid. He was trying to touch me. Frightened of the shape in the bed, I would scream, "Leave me alone, don't touch me." Kicking and punching him I would panic and fly from the bed, smashing my face, bruising my arms or legs as I crashed into the wardrobe or wall to escape this monster. The stranger in my bed reached out to hold me and I fell further into terror. If he tried to pull me back into bed I thought he was going to rape me. The more he came towards me holding his arms out to me, the more afraid of him I was.

Ray was unaware of what was going on in my mind. He didn't know I thought he was a stranger in our bed. He was in fact trying to cuddle and console me, but my interpretation of his gestures was of violence and threatening to me. My mind was so confused that I thought I was going to die, my heart pounded so fast. Eventually I would make my way downstairs to the living room and sit in my chair by the cold fireplace in the dark.

Ray would come down and speak to me through the closed door behind which was a chair to bar his entry. He would go back to bed and, no doubt, cry himself to sleep, I never knew. I would sit with my knees under my chin and my arms wrapped around my legs and rock myself in tears as I returned to reality.

This happened every night for a week or so and Ray learned to leave me alone. No one could do anything for me now. Ray would get up and get the children off to school before shouting goodbye to me through the closed door, waiting a few seconds, but received no reply.

My thoughts were much quieter during the day. I wanted to sleep and never wake up, but I didn't want to die. My bed had become a six-foot square black hole of misery. My bed where Ray and I sipped cocoa and ate digestive biscuits in the first year we were married. The place I left three times to go into hospital to have my lovely babies. The place I lay with my arm through the cot, stroking or gently rocking each tiny miracle that Ray and I were granted from God. Where plans were made for the holidays or a special occasion. Where Christmas morning, three excited children opened their presents. Where on Mothers Day or my birthday a tray with tea and toast was delivered from Ray and the children. Now I sat in my living room all alone, hating my bed, hating myself, hating my life.

Chapter 11

By this time, I knew I had had enough and was tired of it all. The previous week I had spoken to the director of The Samaritans and I admitted to her that I could not go on feeling like this for much longer. Now I began to long for an end to it all. I needed a way of stopping this but there was no way. I couldn't go back and I couldn't go forward. I decided that the only way out was for me to end my life. I got on my bike and rode up to the church. It was unlocked in those days. I walked in and went to the front where the Rector's bible was on his chair. Picking it up I said out loud, "Well God, you know how I feel. I'm sorry, I can't go on any more. I want to be at rest with you."

Then I knelt down and, taking the bible in my hand, I opened it. There in bold black letters on the page in front of me was a paragraph which stood out clearly from the rest on the page. It said "Paul's Prayer. Nothing can separate us from the love of God in Christ Jesus. Not life or death, height or depth, things present or things to come."

I wept bitterly then said, "Oh God, I'm sorry but I know I will never be separated from you."

I got up and went out, got on my bike and started to cycle down towards the steep hill at the end of the road. I peddled fast down the hill and saw a lorry in the distance heading my way. I increased my speed until I was feet away from the lorry, then I closed my eyes and headed straight for it. I heard him sound his horn at me and he swerved and so did I. I flew off over the handle-bars and into a ditch. The lorry never stopped and I sat in the ditch and cried. Then, still weeping, I walked my bike back up to the bottom on the hill, past the school where my three children were, on to my street and home.

I cried and cried, then I rang the curate and told him what I had done. He wanted to come but I said I didn't want him to see me. He made me promise to go to my GP that evening and I said I would.

When Ray came in I told him what I had done and together we went to the doctor's. Ray spoke and I just sat and cried. The doctor asked me what I wanted and I said I wanted to be in hospital because if not, I would kill myself. He said he didn't think I needed to be in hospital. He said that he had known me for around twelve years and he knew that this was just a little depression and he would give me some tablets to help me sleep. Ray agreed and they both said that I could "Pull myself together". But I was too low for that. We went home and I suffered two more nights of even worse hell until I forced Ray to ring the doctor again. This time he told Ray to take me to casualty.

In casualty a young doctor listened to Ray telling him about my depression and how I had tried to run my bike under a lorry. The doctor looked at me and said, "You don't want to go into the Psychiatric ward. Once you do that you will never be out of it. You will use it as an escape every time you want a little break" I just sat and cried. I didn't know what I wanted, I just wanted everything to go away. Eventually at Ray's insistence I was admitted into the hospital.

On the ward I was seen by a doctor and a nurse. The doctor asked me why I wanted to be admitted to hospital. I said that I was confused and needed help. He didn't seem too sympathetic and he pointed to the window and said, "Tell me what you can see when you look out of this window." I looked out and told him I saw the sky, the windows of the opposite building, a gravel path and a tree in the quadrangle beyond the window. He said in a bright and positive tone, "See, you're not confused, you can see clearly." Now I was upset. I cried again because I thought maybe I shouldn't have gone there. Both he and the casualty doctor

A Saint I Ain't

didn't think I needed to be there. Then I had an hour-long session with another doctor who asked me if I was happy at home. He asked about my marriage and the kids. He picked up quickly on my church attendance. I was still unsure now if they thought that I was putting it all on for attention, so I said that I was upset about my mother's death and this changed his line of questions. Then he told me that he was going to give me some strong tablets to make me feel better and I would stay in the ward for a few days to see how I went on. He asked about my sleeping pattern and I said I was staying awake all night and I was tired. He said I would feel much better after some sleep and more food. I realised that I had not eaten for days but I didn't feel hungry.

That night as I lay on my bed I thought about Ray and the children and I sobbed quietly because I felt they must be angry with me for being like this. I soon was asleep but in the early hours of the night, I woke up and heard the voices of people I didn't recognise. They were saying the same things as the people next door. I sat up in bed and put my ear to the wall and I could still hear them.

I burst into tears and got up to go to the sitting room for a cigarette. One of the nurses saw me and asked if I was all right. Like a fool I just said I was all right and didn't tell her about the voices. At the time I knew they were real people but who ever they were, they couldn't have known me. I must have been screaming in the night and they heard me. I thought it was the nurses who were talking about me, but it might have been the patients. They didn't want me to be here. I was taking up a bed and wasting their time, they were saying. I sat in the sitting room all quiet and soon began to feel sleepy; this was the medication they had given me.

The next night it happened again but this time I shouted at them to go away. A nurse came to me and I told her that people were talking about me and I was upset by this. She said it was a dream but I knew it wasn't. I believed people really were talking, I had heard them. I was frightened.

When I next saw a doctor about three days later he questioned me in more depth about my back ground. I told him about our background of neglect and of my father's drinking but I missed out the abuse. I told him about the voices and he said I had to speak to one of the nurses.

I had a named nurse who was to care for me. She asked how I was and I told her about the voices. She said they were not real and I believed her. I said I was mad and she said I wasn't. She said it was the depression that was causing it and it would all go away in time.

After a week I saw the main consultant who seemed to understand. He suggested that I keep a journal, so I did. I was to show this to the nurse and talk through the things I needed to. He also said that he thought ECT (Electroconvulsive Therapy, therapy for treating depression, in which an electric shock is administered to the brain) would help me and would stop the voices which I was still having. I was a little worried about this but he reassured me that, apart from a brief loss of memory immediately after treatment, the side effects were minimal and the full course of five treatments, which he said I would have, would help me recover from the depression much quicker. After discussing this with Ray we agreed and I signed a form and the treatment would begin in a couple of weeks. In the meantime things varied from day to day. The ward routine consisted of group and individual meetings. This combined compulsory relaxation exercises for everyone each mid-morning, which always sent me to sleep, with group discussion in the afternoon, which I hated, then some form of personal recreation around three o'clock. Cards or dominoes were favourites with most of the other patients but I usually did some colouring which I enjoyed. Sometimes a session with my named nurse was slotted somewhere in between. Early morning and evenings we sat fixed to the telly. My smoking increased to an all time high and eating was difficult. I began to bath more regularly. At home I hadn't the energy or desire to care for myself.

At first I would not accept any visitors except Ray. My language skills had taken a sharp decline and holding a conversation was difficult. I also felt that anyone seeing me in this state would think me disgusting. I stammered when I spoke and I shook and twitched nervously day and night. I either repeated myself or didn't manage to finish a sentence with Ray, so talking to other people was something I couldn't face yet.

The day I went to Philip's was Claire's seventh birthday, 24th April 1987. Luke was now twelve and Marie fourteen. We were in the middle of preparing sandwiches and jelly and all the other things that come with a children's party. I had left knowing that, or perhaps because Claire's friends and their mothers as well as my sister in law were coming to the party and I couldn't face it. So I was now feeling terrifically guilty for leaving just when I did. As I said earlier, life was going on all around me and I tried so hard to carry on without anyone knowing. Ray said the people from church, who sent me a big bunch of flowers, were asking about me. They told me later that I should have spoken much earlier, but unless you have been through a breakdown, nobody knows that asking for and even accepting help when it is offered is almost impossible. The one person I did want to see was the curate, who had come when I was having treatment, so I never saw him.

About a month after I was admitted, the ECT began. The first one was scary. I had to put on a hospital cap and gown and, after a pre-med, walked along with four or five others upstairs to the treatment room. When I was called into the room, I got on to a table and the masked doctor and nurse who were gentle and reassuring, gave me another injection. The next thing I knew I was sitting in an arm chair drinking tea in a sort of lounge outside the treatment room. My mind was a blank. I was quiet, clear-headed and only had a very mild headache; no dizziness or sickness usually associated with my being put to sleep. I felt wonderfully calm and placid. Returning to the ward, you have to be told the way as you forget. Even on the ward, I didn't know which was my bed, I had forgotten. It was a strange sensation I remember. But after a little sleep, no more than ten or fifteen minutes, everything came back. After each of the sessions I wrote in my journal and they always were positive and constructive thoughts and feelings. Unfortunately I destroyed this journal years ago. I wish now I had kept it.

In all I was an in-patient for three months. Towards the end I came home at weekends. I was on medication called Prothiaden and without these I would have panic attacks. Some weekends were worse than others, but in all it was good to be home. I was nervous with the children and afraid of the way my friends and neighbours would treat me. I thought they would think I was mad. No one including Ray knew about the voices and now they had stopped. On the 22nd July, our wedding anniversary, I was discharged as an in-patient and was to be seen in the outpatients from then on.

Soon life returned back to normal. I was much calmer now and stayed on medication for a long time. At first Ray and I spoke little about the time of my breakdown. I was very sorry for all the trouble that I had caused and he knew that well enough to have forgiven me for everything I had said and done. There came a time in the weeks before my final inability to cope when I actively and very cruelly tried to make Ray want to throw me out. This was because I hated myself so much for what I was doing, as well as believing at that time that I could never tell Ray about what had happened to me when I was so young. I would sit during the long drawn out days when he was at work and the children were at school, and think about his reaction when he found out that I wasn't a virgin when he met me. For some strange reason known only to my irrational need for self-persecution, I became obsessed with this thought. I believed he would hate me for not saying no, if not to my father, then definitely to all the others who over the years touched or fondled me in unwanted and undesired ways. I should have stopped it. He would think this even if he said he understood. He would lie to make it seem like he didn't care, but he would care, and once he knew he would never forget. Just like I could not forget. The memories locked up in my mind, now as real as the day they happened. Would they never go away?

Occasionally during those days I would suddenly come back to reality and tell myself that Ray would understand and everything would be all right. On those days I would wait for him to come home. The words in my mind were those to tell him everything. Then when he walked in the door and asked me how I was, in a sort of way that says, I daren't ask because I know what she will say. I would fall back into my world again and say blankly, "I'm OK." Then my mind would return to its gloom again and I would go to the bedroom and blame Ray for not asking me in the right way.

Now back home after my long stay in the psychiatric ward, I had to begin to work at building up the broken family I had deserted over the last year or so. I spent lots of time with the children and felt that they were glad to have me back to my old self again. I enjoyed playing with them, talking to them and listening to them. Once again I was interested in what they were doing at home and at school. I got over the large hurdle of going out again. I came to realise that all my friends and neighbours as well as my children's teachers and my Christian friends knew where I had been if not why and that they would not judge me in any way.

Ray was so happy that I was back home and acting so much like my old self again that it would have been easy to leave things just as they were. Once again we enjoyed the time on our own in the evenings. We began to talk as we did before. I was able to communicate with him like the old days. I found the right words to tell him how sorry I was that I had hurt him so much. He had suffered so much pain and misery, and all out of love for me. Words could never express how much I loved him. I told him over the weeks and months everything that had happened to me and, bit by bit, he put together the picture of why and how I went into depression after my mother had died. There was so much to say and he understood everything. In my now rational state of mind I knew that no one could have lived the kind of childhood I had lived and not suffered. I thought that I had survived it well enough to have not let it come between the people I loved and me. But I was wrong.

We spoke about my brothers and sister too. They had let their background show through in so many ways that they were in permanent crisis of one sort or another. I had managed to overcome my upbringing by accepting that I was now in a loving relationship with a man who loved me more than I had ever been loved, and who had allowed me a glimpse of real happiness for the first time in my life. Our three children were the icing on the cake. I had everything going for me.

As well as all this, I also had a firm and true belief in God. This was always something which my family envied me, even when I was at home. My faith had been a comfort to me, but never a prop. It wasn't a way of escape, an unreal dream of heaven with angels, archangels and choirs, where I could imagine only nice things could befall me. No, it was in fact a strength, in that it was faith in God, the one who, in Jesus, was truly human and felt all the pains we humans feel. God was with me in the good times when, as that young lover and new mother, I experienced human love. He was also with me in the dark times when I felt unloved and unlovable.

It took a long time to feel really well again. So much had happened so quickly. But the healing would take much longer than the re-opening of the wounds. About a year after my discharge from my psychiatrist, two major changes were in store for me. The first was my decision to begin work. Ray was now on a good monthly salary. I had been able to manage quiet easily on just his wage up till now. The children were eight, thirteen and fifteen so they were all getting old enough for me to go out to work and leave, even if this overlapped by an hour or two with Ray's shifts occasionally. I would never need to pay a baby-sitter. My self-esteem and confidence had slowly returned and now I needed to do something for myself. I had taken a long time off my Samaritan duties. While I was in such an emotional state I would do more harm than good to both myself and the callers if I had continued. The Director and a couple of Samaritans had

A Saint I Ain't

continued to befriend me and Ray during this time and we were greatly indebted to them for their support. I sometimes spoke to one of them before I told Ray some of the more painful things. Then the words I had to say to him came easier.

I applied for the job of kitchen domestic in a home for the elderly. It was the first job I had tried for since before I was married. I had an interview and was given the job.

At first I was very tired and had very sore and blistered feet. It was hard work and I was on my feet all day long, but I loved it. I was earning my own money to do with what I liked. It gave me such a thrill to be able to buy Ray birthday and Christmas presents out of my own money instead of having to use the housekeeping money as before. Around the same time, Ray and I were talking about me going for Psychotherapy. The sad times in my life were now easier for me to accept, but I still had not dealt fully with the feelings. My psychiatric treatment had dealt entirely with releasing me from the grip of severe depression and talking to Ray and others, I uncovered the facts around why I was as I was. But now it seemed the time was coming when I should look more closely at the feelings around the neglect and abuse from my childhood.

It must have looked from the outsiders' point of view quite an illogical move at this time. I wasn't depressed any more. I had made things right with Ray, the children, and the people at church who I had wronged while I was unbalanced in my mind. I had a job I enjoyed and I was back working as a Samaritan. I was even more confident in my Christian life than I was before and everyone who met me said how well I was looking now. But I was still suffering from what I called nightmares. These were in fact flashbacks from my past. Ray knew how to react by this time. He never tried to touch me when I cried out. We had agreed that he would stay completely still and then I wouldn't try to run from him. It worked, and so when I had them he waited until I controlled myself, then gently asked if I was all right. When it was all over, perhaps only a minute or two after I woke up, I would let him hold me, or sometimes I couldn't and I turned away from him and, curled up in a ball, I would let him go back to sleep, then I would cry quietly so as not to wake him until I fell asleep again. I didn't go to the doctor, as I didn't want medication; I just wanted it to go away. I didn't go back into deep depression, but these nights disturbed me. Sometimes I didn't talk to Ray for days after a bad one. I was embarrassed and annoyed about them and although he never said it, I thought he was afraid, as I was, that it was the beginning of our worst nightmare, serious depression. I found them difficult to handle now that I was supposedly "cured". At these times I still was unable to talk through them which is why we decided that help was needed once more.

I contacted the place where I had already received the information from our former curate who had now moved to another parish. An appointment was made for me to be seen within a week and I went on my own, worried that I was going to set myself back down the slippery road to another breakdown if I started to re-open my vivid memories once more. After an hour-long session, the lady I saw thought, as we did, that psychotherapy would benefit me. The waiting list was however nine months at least so it was a good job that I was reasonably OK. I agreed to begin therapy as soon as a counsellor became available.

In the meantime life went on as usual. We had seen little of my family, keeping contact by phone and Christmas cards on the whole. Philip and Pam came every couple of months and they seemed to be getting along fine. Unfortunately there was a time when Philip became very violent towards her and she feared for her life so they separated for a short time whilst Philip received treatment. Then, after he was put on medication to keep him calmer, they were all right again.

Jill went on to have three more children and she too at times found her quick temper a problem, or rather her husband and children did. Paul visited us less now as his children got older. He too had a quick temper sometimes and I wonder how much blame falls on their childhood. We saw nothing of David and his family.

Robert and June rarely came, and up to this time I had no idea that they had any problems. We phoned one another occasionally and exchanged Christmas cards. Both of them had responsible and full time jobs so I didn't think there was anything wrong in their lives. They, out of all of my family, caused us the least problems and I as always had a special soft spot for Robert. He too loved my three children dearly. He would praise them and say that if he had children, he would like them to be just like mine. I was very proud of them too. In all the years of my depression and throughout and after my breakdown, the children were absolutely marvellous. They never took advantage of the fact that both Ray and I were often occupied with my troubles. They didn't look for extra attention when they might well have done. They too had needs which, while they were never neglected, at times were not met. But throughout it all our family grew stronger. The children were all doing well at school and Ray was still climbing the ladder at work.

My hours at work had increased and now, as well as doing my work as a kitchen domestic, I worked sometimes as a care assistant when the other staff were sick or on holiday. I bought a second hand Honda 90 moped to get me to work and back. This caused mixed feelings with the children. Claire thought it was funny to see mummy on a motorbike. Luke found it cool. Marie however was horrified. Now a teenager and quite the young lady, she said, "If you pass me while I am with my friends I will die of embarrassment." I don't think she approved, but it was just right for me. I loved the feeling of getting on my bike at the crack of dawn when I was on at 6 am, riding to work before the world woke up. I used to hate getting the bus with all the night-shift workers snoozing, and the day-shift workers coughing their lungs up on their morning fag on the way to work.

My bike was handy to get me to the centre to do my Samaritan duty. Here too my hours were slowly increasing as I took on further roles in the branch. My breakdown had released something in me which was meant to be released. I had always been a happy carefree person with all the time in the world for my family and for others. Now it seemed I was even more relaxed than before. If only I could rid myself of the night-time problems I was still having. No one except Ray knew about these. Everyone saw this new boost of youthful energy I had gained, and approved. At work I was dubbed "Evil Kinevil" as I raced into work on my bike. At the Samaritans they said, "Here she comes in her banana suit," as I donned my yellow over suit which I needed on cold winter days.

My priest was not so happy, nor my family for that matter, when I skidded and came off my bike early one morning on my way to work. It was December and I hit a patch of black ice as I approached a roundabout, just minutes from work. The lorry driver who just missed me was more shocked than I was. I flew from my moving bike and we went in opposite directions, me through the air, landing with a crash head-first on the pavement, and my bike skidding right under the lorry. The driver got out to see if I was all right. Luckily we were both going very slowly. It was no one's fault, just road conditions. I was more worried about my bike than me. He stopped my engine and wheeled the twisted bike on to the pavement. Then people had come to see if I needed an ambulance. I felt fine and said no, but asked if I could use the phone in the house nearby. The lady from the house said yes, so I got up to ring Ray to come and pick me and the bike up. It was only when I took my helmet off that I realised I had injured my head and had concussion. My brain felt like jelly. No pain, no cut, just all wobbly and funny. I managed to get into the house and she dialled my number for me. I told Ray and he was off before I had given him the full account. Within ten minutes he was there and insisted that we go to casualty for a check up. I agreed. I did feel a bit queer by then.

The hospital was just across the road from where I worked so as I gave details to the nurse, Ray went across to tell them at work about the accident. I was in with the doctor when he got back. They wanted to cut my suit off, but I wouldn't let them. I unfastened it all and got undressed with the help of the nurse. To her and the doctor's amusement we went through layers of clothing. Being December, it tends to be a bit cold so I always wrapped up well. This padding saved me further injury as well. First was my yellow waterproof suit, my balaclava under the crash helmet and a scarf of course. Then my anorak, under which I wore a thick, quilted, sleeveless waistcoat. Then a thick jumper and a long sleeved blouse under which I wore a t-shirt. On the bottom were my jeans, jogging bottoms under them, two pair of socks and my trainers. "You have to be warm," I told them with a grin. To my horror as I looked down, still obviously in shock and concussed, my elbow looked like it had a tennis ball attached to it. I must have hit the pavement on my arm as well as my head. The doctor said it was broken for sure. I had scraped all the skin off my left upper leg and thigh as well but still I felt no pain. As the doctor wrote out an X-ray form and said he wanted a urine sample to make sure I had no internal bleeding I suddenly remembered something. "Oh no," I cried, "There's a bottle of sherry in my back box, I hope it isn't smashed."

Both the doctor and the nurse laughed at me as I explained that Julie at work had won this bottle of sherry in our church raffle.

"You don't have to explain to us," they sniggered, pretending that they thought I had a drink problem.

Back from X-ray the nurse said they wanted to keep me in for a day or so to keep an eye on me and they were trying to find a bed. The X-ray was clear, no broken elbow, to the amazement of the doctor. It swelled even more and I had a sling on for weeks. They couldn't find a bed so I went home with an appointment to return the next day for a quick check.

At home I was quite ill. My colour drained and my elbow and leg were agony, my ribs hurt too but they had X-rayed all of me, and everything was fine. When our curate came later that day he told me firmly, "No more bikes for you." I told him it was not bad driving - it was ice on the road - but he didn't care, I was banned as far as he was concerned. The bike was a write-off, but I had another within weeks of my injuries healing. Priests can be wrong sometimes.

While I was still recovering, Ray's mum became very ill with pneumonia. She had deteriorated rapidly over the last few months. She had become too confused to care for herself and had to go into the old folks' home near where we lived. She used to wander out, and they had the police looking for her more than once. Now she was very ill and we knew she would not live.

Then Claire had an accident. We were going to the Young Christians, a weekly children's group which I led at church. She skidded on damp grass and dislocated her hip. She was in hospital on traction for months. I went every day. She was still in when, sadly, Ray's mum died. I was extremely upset. To me, she was the dearest person I had known. She was much closer to me than my mother had ever been. We told Claire's doctor but he couldn't take her off the traction even for the funeral. It was so hard for her at accept that her grandma had died, and if she couldn't attend the funeral it would be even harder for her. Anyway, at this time we all wanted to be together. So the doctor let her go home for a few days, then back on traction. We all went to the hospital to be with Claire as often as we could. All three children were always close. Perhaps my illness contributed to that, but it was never a bad thing.

Just before mum went into the home, I heard from the counsellor. It was as they said, nine months ago when I had been first seen. Even though I had many bad nights, the days made up for it. I tried hard not to let the nights sneak into daytime, so as to draw me into depression. For the most part I was successful. During the day my family and work as well as my Samaritan and church activities kept me fully occupied, and I had little time to dwell on myself.

So inevitably, when my first appointment came through, I no longer wanted to do this. I still had the very real fear of actually bringing on depression if I started therapy. I knew I needed it, but I was afraid. I had a lot to lose now. My job would go. My Samaritans work would suffer. We now had a new Rector and curate who weren't around when I had my time in the Psychiatric ward. My children thought I was 100% better now; how would I tell them I needed therapy? The walls were building all around me. I was so afraid. I began to get weepy for the first time in years. Then there he was again - Ray. My strength in all the bad times. Quietly and with sure confidence he encouraged me to see this lady and tell her my fears instead of running away as I had done before. I knew he was right.

It was a good job I had my motorbike. I had a thirty mile round trip to see Gwen, my allotted counsellor. To get there on the bus would take over an hour each way for an hour and a half session. Gwen and I began as far back as I could remember, then I worked my way through the thoughts and memories around the hurts and neglect I had suffered. We always began with the bad things and ended if possible on a lighter note. I was quite comfortable talking to Gwen and she usually just listened. Occasionally she would pick out something and I expanded on it, but most weeks I simply poured out all the things I remembered and told her how I felt about them. It all went very well and I continued to visits her for two years. I was also glad that I had the bike so that often, on the way home, I could stop and take a breather before going home. Nearly every session I ever attended left me feeling emotionally drained. On the way home my head hurt too. It felt like the pressure of slowly releasing steam, but only letting a little out each fortnight, them somehow bottling up the rest and carrying on until the following session. It was much harder than I'd imagined. When I walked into the house I was greeted by the children who wanted to tell me this, that and the other about school. Or, "Have you ironed my PE skirt for morning?" or, "Mum, I'm going on a trip tomorrow, will you pack my sandwiches?"

And Ray had things to tell me about work. I had to switch cold, from re-living bad memories, to the here and now trivia of daily life.

I used to say to Gwen, "I wish I could go away somewhere for a month, do it all, then come back." But it's not as easy as that.

Sometimes I wanted to cry. Gwen had a box of tissues by the side of the chair I always sat in and I used to think, "she's done that so that I will cry, well I won't." So even if I wanted to, I wouldn't cry no matter how bad I felt. I wanted to cry on my way home, perhaps that was why I had the headache, but deep down I told myself that if I allowed the tears to come, they would never stop, so I kept them in. Besides, who was there to cry for? What good would it do? No one listens when you cry.

As the therapy went on, I felt that I was looking at my past in a positive way, which actually surprised me. There were more bad things to remember than good, but even in the bad, I found strangely that some of the worst things were the very things I was using to remind me not to let these things be repeated in my own children's upbringing. This had come naturally to me. Therapy didn't, as I had worried, affect my work, Samaritans, or church life either. Very few people knew that I was having psychotherapy - no one from work, only the director and the few Samaritans who needed to - and no one from church. This was very important to me. I still believed that I was always on the verge of falling back into depression and inevitably to suicidal thoughts again. I spoke to Gwen about my worries and she reassured me that if I did feel too bad, we would stop and have a rest.

The time came, about eighteen months into the therapy, when we began to touch on my recent breakdown, and things changed. I was feeling the pressure of re-opening the feelings around my breakdown. I began to suffer the night terrors three and four times a week and I was really scared. I wanted to run away all the time. I couldn't talk to Ray about it and I wasn't fully honest with Gwen. I began to have flashbacks from the past, which was of serious abuse that I hadn't remembered. I was afraid to tell Gwen because I thought she would think that I was making it up to make things more dramatic. So I bottled it all up. I began to blame Ray. I thought he was doing things to me while I was asleep and this was what I was feeling. This wasn't true, but I had to have an answer. Why, after all I had been through, both psychiatric and psychotherapeutic treatment, were things getting worse, not better? I used cider to get myself to sleep so I wouldn't wake up and feel all these unpleasant things happening to me. Whether they were real or imaginary I didn't know now, I just wanted them to stop. Eventually I told Gwen and we talked about my need to run away. I told her of the times I had thought about ending my life, usually during the night after a flashback when I saw no end to my misery. I described how I imagined I would buy a bottle of whisky, take it into a field far away from the road, then take the tablets that I would store up with the whisky, and die. I didn't want to be found, it wasn't a cry for help. I wanted to die. For a short time she saw me weekly until we worked through my feelings. I never told Ray and had to come home each week feeling sad and very guilty that I was feeling so bad and couldn't talk to him about it. I agreed with Gwen that I would write down how I felt immediately the flashbacks were over, so I kept a pad of paper and a pen by my bed and would write or even draw how I felt and what I saw. This time it was different. On the way home from Gwen's I cried and cried. Often I stopped on the long empty road and looked into the distance, alone and in despair again. When will it end, I asked myself through the tears. Now I didn't want to kill myself, I wanted to be free. I didn't want to run away, I wanted to be happy again. At home I felt all right. Things were going well now. The children were less demanding now they were older. I had enjoyed each stage of their growing up so far and now I was feeling that they too were beginning to mature into young adolescents, each with their own wonderful characteristics.

Marie had overcome her illness and accepted the limitations brought about as a result of the arthritis left from the rheumatic fever. She was working hard at college and was on her way to applying to university. She was strong-headed but firm and dependable, well-liked by her peers and tutors. Luke had been through a traumatic last year of secondary school and was going on to sixth form college. He was a sensitive young man who cared deeply for environmental issues and was into music in a big way. Claire was ready to begin her secondary education and she loved music, both playing and listening, and said she wanted to look after children when she left school.

I was still enjoying working at the old folks' home in the kitchen. I never discussed my home or family problems with anyone at work. They saw me as completely together and would have been surprised if they knew a quarter of what was going on in my mind and my life. At the Samaritans I had begun to say less to the couple of people who knew about my problems. I was now holding some responsible positions and I didn't want them to think that I couldn't cope. If they asked how I was I said I was fine and they saw no reason to doubt this. At church I now had a very good spiritual director. He was a priest in Doncaster who I met with regularly and spoke about my Christian life as well as being able to tell him all about the things I discussed with Gwen. He heard my confessions too so he, most of all, knew my innermost thoughts and there were times when without him, I thought I would not have been able to cope.

Somehow I managed to balance my therapy, my Christian life and my personal and family values and get through every day with an outward show of composure and still have the strength to support and care for others with only a few knowing that I was battling with my past. In 1990 I came to the end of my therapy. I was now fully over the feelings of wanting to run away. I had worked through the suicidal thought period and through accepting in my heart that I had not been wrong to have the feelings of being let down by both my parents all my life. I now was coming out of that long dark tunnel you hear about. I could now say without feeling guilty that I could not forgive my mother. Especially for her not giving me the childhood I deserved. I had come to believe that she was as much a damaged adult as she had made her six children. However, this held no comfort to me when I realised how close I had come to repeating history and making my husband and children's lives a misery because of her. I had gone from hating her to pitying her. Now I just felt nothing for her and that would have to be enough at the moment.

Chapter 12

The next couple of years went by relatively problem-free. Ray and I were much happier again. We spent a lot of time talking now and this was good for both of us. It now seemed that my mother's death had helped me to face the things in my past which should have been dealt with many years ago. I still have to say that these things had not spoiled my life in any way up to now. They must have been so deep-rooted that I truly had forgotten them until her death, or rather the reaction of my brothers and sister at her death, opened up these feelings that were there anyway. All the fun came back into my life again. I enjoyed the children more than I had ever done. I still hadn't told them about my past, it wasn't necessary to tell them anything. They were now all three very mature youngsters and this in itself was proof that my breakdown hadn't affected them too badly. Perhaps one day I would tell them, but at that time there was no need.

Our holidays were once again fun times and weekends and evenings which I had dreaded over the last few years were now times of pleasure. I began to restore the house to its former cleanliness. I was never super-mum, but I did care for my house and family with the love they deserved. All this had to be rebuilt slowly. Philip, Paul, Jill and David continued to have many problems. Occasionally, with Ray's support, we did help them, but as a rule we left them to sort their own problems out now. I wasn't going to let anyone spoil the hard work we had put into

A Saint I Ain't

my recovery, especially as they never seemed to improve as each crisis came and went for them or their family. Ray and I had dealt with all ours as well as theirs, now they were on their own. As ever, Robert and June, his wife, seemed to be fine and never unloaded anything on to us like the rest.

As well as my private and social life improving, my spiritual life took a big leap forward too. Ray had continued to climb his working ladder as well. We went to works' dinners and socials together and in the summer I went along to watch him play cricket. He started going fishing and enjoying other hobbies once again. His life had been stunted as much as mine, but in a different way. Life would never be the same, but for the better I have to say.

Soon everyone forgot the bad days we had suffered. Our friends and family, neighbours and workmates, either never knew, didn't care or presumed we had worked everything out. Life was happy and normal again. I still had some bad nights but on the whole I coped with life as it came. I felt like a new person again. I thought nothing could ever be as bad as the last ten years.

The little things in life were once again a treasure to me. I have always had a deep love of nature. I love the countryside and the coast equally. In February 1991 our curate, who had been with us since 1989, left to go to a new parish in London. Our family would miss him, as we had become close to him, not only in the church life but outside and socially. He was very kind to us all when we were all in need of special care and attention. He had seen us through Claire's long stay in hospital, she loved him to visit her. He was wonderfully kind during and after Ray's mum's death and funeral. Ray could talk to him, they got on very well, and we often went out for a drink to the quiz night at the local pub. Luke and Marie liked him a lot because he was young and trendy and they saw him as a friend as much as a priest. We helped him too by looking after his dog, a large sloppy Boxer dog called Tanya. When he went on holiday and sometimes on his day off, she would stay with us. She was almost part of the family and we would miss her as much, if not more than we missed him when the time came for them to go. We still receive photos and news updates of her from him, and Ray and I still ring or visit him when we can. Sadly the Church of England lost a good priest when he resigned in '92 following the Women Priest vote, but that's another story.

On Palm Sunday 1992, the Rector announced to our congregation that a decision had been made by the Bishop and the pastoral committee that we were to become separate from the parish church. We were to have a priest of our own. This was welcomed by all the congregation. Throughout all this time, I was meeting with my spiritual director because God was speaking to me in a very real and special way, showing me things through scripture and prayer and in the sacraments, guiding me through a tough spiritual journey. This, I see now, was the beginning of my ministry in the church. This was not Ministry to Holy Orders, I wasn't being called to be a priest, but quite clearly to minister to others both inside and outside the church in a pastoral role. Only my spiritual director and Ray knew about this. It was tested and proved right on numerous occasions.

Then fate dealt me another disastrous blow. My working life was changing. The home where I was working was to close and we were to merge, with two other homes, to make one big home. All our staff and most of the residents would move to Oakdale, which was the site of the old hospital and had been totally redesigned and made into this wonderful brand new home.

In January 1991 we had a two-week induction course for all the staff who would run this home. I attended as a Kitchen Domestic. The home was furnished with the best and most modern furniture in the lounges, dining areas and bedrooms. The staff were encouraged at all times to respect the privacy and personal dignity of the residents. They were to spend as much time as possible interacting with them and not, as had been seen in other homes, simply to get them up, wash, dress and feed them, then sit them in a lounge until the next meal, then put them to bed. This home would be different. They, and their relatives, would be encouraged to communicate with the staff and with one another. There were nurses, a hairdresser, chiropodist, physiotherapists, occupational therapists and others to care for their mental as well as physical needs. Each room was single with matching duvet and curtains. There was even a double bed for one married couple. The kitchen was in the basement. It was fitted with the very latest equipment. The meals went up in the lift to the dining areas in hot trolleys and special diets were given for many of the residents. Only the best and freshest fruit and veg was used. The menus were the most up-to-date and healthy choices to encourage good appetites. I still enjoyed being a kitchen domestic. Even the washing-up and scrubbing the work surfaces and floors was a pleasure in this home. Sometimes, when the cook was off ill or on holiday, I came in on her shift and did the cooking. The menus were easy to follow and the modern kitchen equipment made cooking easier.

I was really happy now. Life as a whole was definitely looking up now, apart from the changes at church, but this got better eventually. I still had my motorbike for work and each day I loved going to work. The family were virtually independent of me now. I was even asked to be one of the deputy directors at the Samaritans, a post I was able and willing to accept. Now my depression and breakdown were a distant memory. I came to be thankful that they had happened. I realised that because of them, I now felt more confident. I was able to be completely honest and felt more sincere with Ray, something that was very important to me. I could be truthful and open with my priest as well now. Most important was that I was honest and absolutely genuine as a person now that I had been able to free myself from all the guilt that I had attached to myself. I had lived all my life feeling responsible for the things I did and the things that were done to me. Now that I was free from these self-imposed and obsessive feelings of guilt, I could begin a new process of development. And the best thing was, still very few people knew. People always saw me as dependable, happy, relaxed and carefree and in truth I hadn't really been all these things, but now I could be. I could be myself at last. It was truly a liberating feeling. Sometimes on my bike on the way to work, I would become exhilarated at the way my fortunes had turned out. I was glad to be alive and free. I loved life and I loved everyone including myself. People at work used to laugh at my enthusiasm for everything I did. In church I showed a very quiet side of me. I was feeling regenerated in my spiritual life. Here I found peace and tranquillity. At one with God and man as it were. It all felt so new and wonderful. Life had meaning again and with it came power, which made me a little afraid of what God might have in store for me. This self-confidence and renewed self-esteem made me feel clean inside and out.

In June 1991 I moved from the kitchen to be a care assistant. The staff had said my caring ability was wasted in the kitchen so I was encouraged to apply for a care job which was vacant. After an interview with my boss Tina and the area manager, I was given the job of Care Assistant. Now I was even happier to be at work. I enjoyed looking after the old folk, and they liked me. I got on well with the other care staff and things couldn't get any better. We had an electronic organ in one of the open lounges and sometimes when I was on afternoons, I would play some of the old songs like "Knees up Mother Brown" and their favourite hymns, and both residents and their relatives liked to sing along. This left the other staff free to bath or put to bed some of the residents. We all had fun, and at the same time it helped the smooth running of the home.

In January 1992 my happy world came to an abrupt halt. I was on a day shift which was 6 am till 2 p.m. It was the very end of the shift and I was walking through to join the handover with the afternoon shift when one of the residents asked me to take her to the toilet. I should have said, 'No, wait five minutes until the next shift comes on,' but I didn't. I called to a colleague and asked her to help me. This particular resident was a very large lady weighing at least sixteen or seventeen stone. We all had

A Saint I Ain't

difficulty lifting her. She was on a diet but the weight stayed on. It didn't help that she had lost the use of one side of her body after a severe stroke so she wasn't mobile enough to work off the weight. She wore a leg iron on one leg and found standing impossible. She asked to be taken to the toilet more frequently than most. It always took two people to lift her. I went for a wheelchair for her, and my colleague and I began to get her to her feet. As we were turning her towards the wheelchair, she slipped and fell back into the armchair. My colleague let go of her side of the lady and I automatically held on. As she fell sharply, I twisted my back as her weight took me down with her. I felt an extremely sharp pain in the middle and base of my back, and then a crack. I have never suffered from back pain or had a back injury so I thought it would just stop hurting after a few minutes. My colleague called someone else to lift with her and they took the lady to the toilet. I stood against the lounge wall in great pain, waiting for it to ease. Then when they had got her back to her chair we went into the staff room right at the end of hand-over. I stood against the back wall, pressing my back to the wall to relieve the pain. No one knew what had happened except me and the other two who had lifted the lady. I didn't tell any of the staff in charge as I should have done, but at that time I thought it would stop hurting and I would be back for my next shift the following day. If it had happened earlier on in the shift things would have been different. As it was right at the end of the shift, I went home without reporting it as an accident. Luckily for me, Ray was off that day and, as he always did on his day off, he had taken me to work in the car to save me going on my bike in the freezing cold. He was there at two o'clock that afternoon to take me home in the car. It was a good job too. I could never have got on my bike, the pain was so bad. Still I thought I would be back at 6am the next day.

We pulled up at home and I struggled up the grass verge and into the house. The pain was bad, but bearable. Then I lifted my leg to step over Marie's keyboard which was on the living room floor and something snapped in my back and I fell onto the settee. The pain was excruciating. I screamed in agony and as soon as I settled on the settee, Ray called my GP. The receptionist said that the doctors were in surgery and she would ring him back. Within a few minutes she rang back and told him that the doctor had rung a prescription through to our local chemist and he was to pick it up. She said if it got no better, we were to ring in the morning. The tablets he got were Proximol, but they did no good at all. Then work rang to ask me to work an extra shift and he told them about the accident. I spent the night on the settee, unable to move an inch the pain was so bad. I couldn't sit up and even moving my head sent pain down my back.

The next day Ray sent for a locum to see me. When he examined me he said it looked like a slipped disc and rest would help. He gave me some Diamorphine to take and said that if I could get upstairs, I was to put a board under my mattress and stay flat for as long as I needed to, until the pain subsided. It took me until Sunday to attempt the stairs. Ray and Luke helped me upstairs but the pain reduced me to tears. It upset them as well, it was so bad. Once in bed, I would remain there. On Monday we sent for my doctor who agreed with the locum that I had a slipped disc and bed rest would cure it. I told him about the lifting accident and he gave me a sick note for a month. He also gave me a prescription for valium to help me to relax and more strong pain killers. I stayed in bed for two or three weeks and the pain did settle if I stayed completely still and flat on my back. Friends from work came to see me and they brought me flowers and were very kind. Some Samaritans came to see me, and friends from church. Time dragged as I lay in bed unable to move. Around a month after the accident Ray rang an osteopath. When Ray told him the history he told Ray to get a bag of frozen peas from the freezer and wrap them in a tea towel and, with me on my tummy, place the ice pack in the site of the pain and he reassured us that, after fifteen minutes, I would be able to get up. It worked and I went to his office to receive treatment. It helped me a lot at the time, but soon the pain would come back. I went for a couple of months and this did help me to get mobile again.

The following twelve months is a blur of good and bad episodes of back pain, ranging from bad to severe. I had weeks in bed or on the settee on a board, and other times when I coped with the pain. At times I got very depressed. In June, just six months after the accident, I had to go for a medical from work. The outcome was a letter saying I was unfit to do my job so I was sacked. In August I went to see a solicitor to claim unfair dismissal. He said he thought from what I told him of the accident, that I had cause to claim that my employers were negligent. They should have provided lifting equipment for this lady. We used a hoist to get her up in the mornings, but we weren't allowed to use it during the day. It was designed only for lifting her out of bed. I talked to Ray and others about my worries about suing the my employers. Everyone said the same as the solicitor. I agreed to carry on with the case. I wanted to be pain free. I knew that my back could go at any time. Sometimes in the early days simply opening a drawer or stretching to reach something left me flat on my back for days. Dressing and undressing and bathing were mammoth tasks now. I would lie on my bed and think and get very down. It seemed to me that all the emotional pain I had suffered in recent years and the all too brief glimpse of a new carefree and happy family life for me, Ray and the children had now gone forever. I missed work so much, both the residents and my friends. I loved being a care assistant and now they didn't want me. I missed church too. I couldn't go very often and when I did I couldn't sit to play the organ which I loved doing. I missed my motorbike and the freedom it gave me. In a fit of temper and frustration I sold both my bike and the elctronic organ I played at home. Just seeing them made me upset.

In all this time I never got into serious depression though. I was quite justifiably angry at the situation I found myself in. I was sad and felt lonely and unwanted. Workmates stopped calling. Church friends stopped visiting and when I was better, they replaced me with another organist which was quite right. The family got on with their lives. I saw more of Ray's relatives than mine. That was what I expected. My family took from me, but they didn't give. I did see Robert and June who were very supportive to me and the family.

Soon my case against my employers began to take shape. I was sent to see a consultant orthopaedic surgeon and had X-rays and a medical. The X-ray showed little, but it was now a year since the accident and things had settled. I could just cope with the pain if I didn't lift anything or walk too far or bend and I was careful standing and sitting. My daily life was ruled by the managing of my pain.

In September 1992 our new priest came to our little church. The people of the church prepared the house for the arrival of its first priest in charge. His induction was a grand occasion which was attended by many priests from the diocese and family and friends of our new priest. At first the enthusiasm of both priest and people was great, but alas it would not be for long. A combination of the many small but significant signs showed that there were going to be problems for the parish and its priest. Then in November came the thing we feared most. The vote was passed to accept women for ordination. Many priests I knew left the Church of England. Some joined the Roman or Orthodox church while others gave up their priestly ministry. Our new priest took the vote to be the last straw and so began long periods of his time off work due to ill health. One of those who left after the vote was my spiritual director from Doncaster.

My injury still caused me great pain and I was limited in all ways. By early 1993 I had slowly rejoined the Samaritans but found travelling to the centre on the bus, then the walk up to the centre, very painful. Anyone with a bad back will appreciate how difficult bus journeys are. Until then I had never had problems on a bus, but now, simply getting on and off was agony. But in my more determined moments when I was not going to be beaten, I battled through. Soon I began to take driving lessons again. I picked up quickly where I had left off before I gave up and went to the motorbike. After a few lessons and one failed test, I passed on the second test. This would help me to regain a little more independence when I needed it. Ray was very good and would always take me anywhere if I asked him, but owning my own car would be brilliant. Ray bought me a cheap ten year old mini which was my wheels to freedom, no more painful bus travel.

My case had taken a new turn. I had seen the report from my medical expert, the orthopaedic surgeon. I was amazed at how unsupportive he was - not so much about my present injury, he reported that the evidence showed damage to the lower three vertebra, which corresponded with my injury. But then he went on to say that this may have been an old injury or simply degenerative changes - in other words, the ageing process. Then he went on to pick all the negative things from my medical history, after seeing all my GP and hospital notes. When I expressed my worries to my solicitor, he said that the case was not very strong anyway so he was not very optimistic. This led me to ask for a second opinion. I went to see a big city firm of solicitors who, after seeing all the evidence from my previous solicitor, took my case on. It would be a long and a difficult case and, as Ray was on a good salary, we didn't qualify for legal aid. It would be an expensive case I was told. After long deliberations, Ray and I agreed to go ahead.

Two years after my accident and I was reaching the conclusion that the pain was going to remain with me no matter what I did. So, being the fighter I am, I told myself that I would not give in and sit in a corner crying, I would do all I could to live my now limited life to the fullest I could manage. I did as much as I could in the way of house work, but inevitably the house had begun to look neglected. I was fed up with pestering the family to keep it clean, so week by week the task of housekeeping was less of a worry to me. I still had a happy marriage and the children were happy. Why should I let a bit of muck and dust worry me, I told myself as the windows got left and the curtains changed less frequently. The ironing was done by whoever wanted to wear ironed clothes. If they weren't bothered, why should I be? Life's too short to let housework shorten it, I thought. I did the necessary jobs and left the others. This improved my mobility bit by bit. I would not be beaten. One of my main problems was finding a comfortable position in bed. Sleep got less and less as I would wake every two or three hours in severe pain. We bought an orthopaedic bed and this helped a little. It became such that what I did during the day, exercise-wise, determined how well I slept and how much pain I suffered the next day. Still I did all I could to keep active in mind and body. I used to remind myself that I was lucky that the children were grown up. If I'd had toddlers to push and pull, I would never have coped. Now our children were becoming independent of us both.

We were very proud when Marie gained a place at Oxford. Luke had now started to work as a chef and was living in a flat near his work. Claire began to look at her options for her GCSEs at school.

Ray had been worried when a new company bought British Steel where he worked. Everyone had to re-apply for their own jobs. Hundreds would be made redundant. It looked certain that he would lose his job. After a long negotiation with management, he was encouraged not to take his redundancy money, but to accept a small percentage of his wages for eighteen months and do a degree course at University which would give him the qualifications to teach engineering. He accepted this. His salary stopped and his firm paid his first term at University. Certain clauses meant all our major debts would be paid. However, within six months, things went wrong and we lost everything they had promised him. He was on the dole. He had trusted others who failed us. Times would get very hard, but as we were a solid couple and our marriage was still strong, we pulled through. It was at this time that I started to be very angry because had it not been for the accident, I should have been able to contribute financially in place of Ray. He had worked all his life and never been on the dole. Now in his early '40s the prospects of a job for him were slim. He remained unemployed for two years. Luckily, before Ray lost his job, I had changed my car. I now had a more reliable Fiat Panda. We now were unable to afford two cars so Ray sold his and we shared the Panda. This worked fine. Neither of us went far so we rarely clashed, and each of us had it when we wanted it.

Our church life, which was so important to us, became difficult. Things were changing in our church. There came a time when we had to minister to our Priest. His illnesses were longer these days. God had continued to speak clearly to me in the scriptures and sacraments of the church. I made my confessions regularly and went as often as I could on retreats and quiet days, always eager to listen to God in prayer. Although our lives had seen so many changes over the recent years, both Ray and I found comfort and strength in our faith. We used every situation to the best of our ability. Even when things were looking at their bleakest, we had a positive approach. We couldn't deny that some problems were insurmountable, so we learned to cope as best we could, finding the good in all.

Money was always top of our worry list. Before Ray found work, I had to go for a medical and my Invalidity money was stopped. This was devastating. Ray was so desperate, he would have taken any job. He applied for everything in the papers that he felt he could do, but nothing came for him.

Chapter 13

Robert and June began to have serious problems. Robert's drinking had got so bad that June couldn't cope and for the first time ever, she confided in us that he had been steadily getting worse for years. At this time, she knew nothing of our childhood. She, like Ray, knew that we had an alcoholic father and that our mother couldn't cope. Robert never spoke about it.

By coincidence at the same time another of my brothers turned up one evening, absolutely drunk, saying that he could not go home until he stopped drinking. Once again, Luke willingly gave up his bedroom so that his uncle could stay for a while. That night he went to bed and slept off the booze. We all agreed about having him until he stopped drinking, then we let his family know he was with us and that we would try to help him to dry out.

We said two weeks would be our limit. After that he would have to go back home. Within forty-eight hours we saw for the first time the true effect of coming off alcohol. This was very unpleasant for him and for us. He was confused, had hallucinations, vomited. He drank gallons of water to quell a severe thirst. On the third day he was so ill that I took him to my GP. When the doctor saw him he knew what to do. He gave him medication to ease the symptoms. This worked straight away. It meant explaining to my doctor some of our history, we had both suffered badly from the abuse and neglect from our childhood. After about six days he began eating normally and came downstairs in the evenings and joined us. One night he said he wanted to speak to me about our childhood and the things which had happened to him, which he was covering up with drinking. We talked into the night and we both presumed that Robert may have the same need to talk. The next day I rang June and told her that we were coming to see Robert. When we arrived she went out and left the three of us alone. We talked of things we had never disclosed before, not even to one another. My brother left us that week and remained off the booze for a time, but he did start again. Robert said he too would stop drinking and face his past sober. Sadly this was not to be.

My solicitor was racing on with the case now. I had been seen by many experts and they all were to prepare statements to put to my employers' solicitors. I saw medical experts, an employment consultant, even a clinical psychologist. Each time I saw one for my solicitor, my employers solicitors would send me to be examined by one of their own experts whose report would say the opposite of mine of course. At times this got to me. Strangers were finding out some of the most personal and intimate details of my background. It was bad enough when they were on my side, but some of the reports from their experts upset me. At the time I expressed my concern to my solicitor and he was most understanding. However, at home, or more usually in the quiet of my empty church, I cried more than I had done even during my breakdown. I didn't let it get me down too much, but occasionally I wanted to run away. But then I would speak to Ray and I would be all right.

1995 was to be year which must go down in my history as being one of the toughest I was to endure. January began with my leaving the church I had attended for nearly twenty years. This had been a hard decision for me to make. It began the previous year and now it was time to put into practice what I believed God wanted of me. I say what He wanted, as it surely wasn't what I wanted. I found it difficult to leave the place where I was baptised and brought to faith and where all my family worshipped. Change is never easy. It meant finding another place to receive the sacraments. I decided to go to St Mary's and see how things went from there. I missed my friends at the old church and I still do, but I was meant to be at St Mary's, for the time being at least. Within months of going there, I began the two year Pastoral Worker Course. This opened up many new things in my knowledge and understanding of what ministry is and how to be useful in a practical way in church life and the community. I would never have been given this opportunity at my old church.

Other things made me realise that I had made the right decision. My prayer life and spiritual direction are much improved. I can now express more easily and freely what I feel God is showing me. This can only be good. There are however some things that will never be the same for me. While all this was going on in my church life and with my case was getting nearer to its conclusion, I was asked if I would consider taking on the role of Director at the Samaritan branch where I had been a volunteer for eleven years. I was extremely honoured to have been even considered for such a role. After due thought and discussion with my family, I said I would take it on. It was to be a three year post, after which I would stand down to allow another Director to take over. My back pain shouldn't be affected by doing this job. If I had a very bad day and the pain was very intense, I could delegate anything I needed doing to one of the four deputies I had chosen. I felt confident and privileged and would take over from the present Director at the AGM in May. This gave me three months to prepare. Then, in the same week that I was asked to be Director, another problem was to rear its head.

Towards the middle of the previous year and into that year we had much more contact with Robert and June. Robert was now much worse. His drinking was making him ill and mentally he was a nervous wreck. June continued to work and Robert took early retirement through ill health. He had counselling and therapy and went into hospital to dry out. But he carried on drinking and getting more and more depressed. He was never loud or angry, he simply sat in his bedroom and drank his life away, often sleeping for days, then waking to drink more. June came to see us one day on her own. She was at the end of her tether. She was working round the clock and getting less sleep, as Robert stayed up through the night and slept when she was at work. They had begun to have heated arguments now and she could take no more. After a long time she broke down and said they would have to split up if something wasn't done. No one wanted this. She still loved Robert but life with him was unbearable. She also knew that he was completely unable to look after himself. Ray said straight away that he could come and stay with us until he dried out. The problem would be if Robert didn't want to come. We left it that June would tell him he could stay with us until he was able to find his own place. She said she wanted a year-long separation so that she could be sure he had stopped drinking. He also had to agree to get help from AA or some other agency. In the past he had promised so many times. Now he must do it if he valued his marriage. Robert agreed to all this and he moved in with us. There was just Claire living at home now. Marie was still at Oxford and Luke had his flat in town.

We saw Robert go through the same trauma as his brother. Withdrawal was hell for us all. This time I went to see my GP with Robert before he started to suffer. Nevertheless it was longer and harder for him. Eventually he did recover and began to enjoy a new lease of life. June had told him that he was not to contact her even after the withdrawal. She too needed some peace. We felt for her so much. She was alone and missed him terribly. She and Robert had no children. Robert had always said that because of his damaged childhood, he felt unable to cope with a family of his own. I rang her regularly to give her news of Robert's progress and to see how she was coping. She felt very guilty and thought that, although we seemed to support her, we must blame her in some way. We reassured her that not only did we not blame her, but that we thought she had done a marvellous job so far showing such patience and tolerance in an unenviable situation.

Robert moved in with us, after which he went into an Alcohol

Rehabilitation Centre. He agreed to live there for six months to get over the drinking, then he would get a place of his own. After only a month in the centre he decided that he was ready to live on his own. Reluctantly the centre let him leave when he agreed to spend each day with them, continuing through the drying-out programme which took six months. Ray and I found a flat near the centre and we helped him to get the furniture together. Money was not a problem as Robert had his own income, separate from June. Things went well for a few weeks, then Robert decided that he had done so well that June should let him stay at their home at weekends. As with his rehab, he went too fast too soon and he started to drink again. He was found to have drink on him in the rehab centre so he was asked to leave. Robert wanted to give up his flat and go back to June. He made promises we all knew he couldn't keep. June wouldn't let him stay with her so he went down quickly and soon he was back to a bottle of whisky and at least three litres of red wine each day. When he was drunk, he would ring June and upset her. I went each day to his flat to find him drunk in bed. He didn't eat anything at all. His only intake was alcohol, the amount increasing each day. After a month or so we did take him back home with us and he dried out and went back to the centre for a while, but this was not to last. By May I was ready to take over as Director of the Samaritans. We had tried not to let Robert and June's problems stop the daily running of our lives. At times this was hard. Marie, Luke and Claire loved Uncle Robert and helped in every way to give him the support he needed. Also in May, the same week as I took over as Director, I had my first visit to a pain clinic to have treatment for my back pain. I had been on the waiting list for over nine months by then and finally the first visit had come.

At the clinic the pain management team included a nurse, a top consultant, a physiotherapist who did manipulation, and a clinical psychologist who helped me accept the long term effects of the pain. Together they decided what kind of treatment would help each patient to manage their pain to get the best out of life. I

A Saint I Ain't

would go fortnightly at first, then each month from then on. The treatment turned out to be of great benefit to me. Not all patients respond as well as I did - all pain is different, depending on the root cause.

The Samaritan AGM was a nerve-racking evening for me. The role of Director was a rewarding, if a demanding one. I worried more about my health than my ability to do the job. My back could go at any time so I was always careful to avoid stairs, steps and lifting at all times.

Robert had remained sober long enough to move to a flat near his home. This was against the advice of rehab people, myself and June. We all knew he was making himself so ill that soon he would have liver damage. He had made many suicide attempts and he was not capable of caring for himself. June now had the task that I had been carrying out. Each day she would call in and see him in his flat. Every day she would find him unconscious in bed or on the settee. She rang me often to share her concerns. One Friday night in the last week of May, June rang in a terrible state. What we all feared had happened. She had found him dead on the bedroom floor. He had choked on his vomit and never regained consciousness. He died alone. I contacted one of my deputies and told her I would be off for a few weeks, then Ray and I went to be with June.

Robert's death hit all our family very badly. The funeral a week later was packed with many of his friends from work as well as all our family and June's and some from the Alcohol Advice Service and the rehab centre. The day after the funeral I went for my second visit to the pain clinic. As soon as they asked me how I was, I broke down in tears and told them about Robert. They let me cry for a long time, then I just went home.

The week after his death, June and I went to their chalet in Mablethorpe where they had spent many happy times. She wanted to scatter his ashes at Mablethorpe and she asked if I would be with her as she carried this out. I agreed for June's sake and this gave her great comfort. We spoke a lot on the journey down. June was eager to know as much about Robert's early years as she could. I told her about the time me and the boys went up the lanes near where we lived to play our game of pretending to shoot the passing traffic with our pretend guns. I was very much a tom-boy of course, keeping up with the boys as ever. On this occasion they pulled, pushed and tugged me right up to the top of the tree where I balanced precariously on the thin end of a branch. The boys proceeded to slip quickly down the tree leaving me screaming and crying as they laughed at me from the roadside. They left me until it was getting dark before they finally rescued me. And there was the time we raided the farmer's field and sold potatoes to one of the neighbours, using the money to buy liquorice torpedoes. The year they dressed me up as a Guy Fawkes, sitting me outside the Working Man's club in Philip's pram and got money out of the drunks. June laughed at my tales, but I had a lump in my throat as big as an apple. In the boot in a cardboard tube was the remains of one of the most important people in my life; the one who had given me away on my wedding day; the one who had bought a teddy for Claire which was bigger than she was. My brother who, just weeks earlier, in few hours of semi-sober conversation, had shared intimate moments of memories only we could speak of when he had told me he was sorry for things he had done when we were younger. Words he needed to say and that I needed to hear.

I was sorry he and June had split up so near to the end of his life, but I was glad of the year we had spent as the brother and sister that were trying to make amends for our tragic missed childhood. I will never forget buying curtains and crockery, pictures for the walls and ornaments and plants to decorate his little flat. It was not all for nothing. He died as he would have wanted it, without anyone seeing him in the pain and agony he was suffering emotionally and physically. He could never come to terms with the conditions he had lived in as a child and now the adult Robert could no longer bear to face the future. No one could cure Robert, his death was inevitable, and he would not have wanted June or me to see him die.

A Saint I Ain't

Following his death, myself and Ray and the children went through a bad few weeks. Anyone who knew Robert knew a gentle, loving, caring man, a gentleman in every way. Only in the last bitter pains of his addiction did this side of him slip into the background for a while. We would miss him. I wept most evenings when I thought of the waste of a life. The feelings of hatred of my parents returned. I spoke to my parish priest of my unwillingness to forgive, especially my mother. I accused God of neglecting us too. If he had been there in the darkest times of our childhood, why had he allowed such suffering to continue in the lives of innocent children? My priest allowed me to release all my feelings and supported me through the bad time, never once condemning me or telling me I couldn't or shouldn't feel this way. My cries were raised in grief and I was hurting so much I hated God. I would look at myself in my bedroom mirror. I stared hard and coldly into my own eyes at times to try to see myself as others see me. Loved and loveable, well I didn't think I was. For a brief moment I would want to be with Robert, then I knew that I was wrong. I had a life to live, if only to prove that they, my parents, would not ruin my life as they had the others in my family. I soon picked myself up, dusted myself down and began to get back to the realities of my life.

The work at the Samaritans had continued as my four deputies shared the responsibilities between them, consulting me when they needed to. I had received tremendous support since Robert's funeral, but now I must take over once again and start to plan the way I was to run the branch over the next three years as Director. It would be wrong to say I threw myself into it to cover up my sorrow and grief, but it did help that I could build on the caring side of my nature, helping the seventy volunteers in the branch to give the best possible service to the callers who needed them.

The Director's job is primarily to care for and support the volunteers so that they are better equipped to help those that contact us. It involves keeping our building open, manned and in good running order, so fund-raising, publicity and outreach all play their part. Within a week of taking over I had my photo in the local paper when I received a large cheque for the centre. This caused raised eyebrows from friends and neighbours who never knew that I was a Samaritan, let alone the Director of the branch. But fame never went to my head and I actually began to enjoy the role in a way I had not expected. Being in charge doesn't mean you have to be bossy or a bully, it demands control and when decisions have to be made, and seeing them through. Sometimes the decisions and changes I made were not easy, but I always relied on others to help me both in the branch and regionally.

In October the same year I began the Pastoral Workers Course. This was to be a big turning point in my learning about putting my faith into practice. There were around one hundred on the actual course, but these were broken down into manageable groups who would remain together throughout the two year course. There were eleven in my group and we were all from different church backgrounds. Most were from evangelical parishes and soon we saw that there was a wide spectrum between this and my catholic background. We all respected the others' differences. One of the main things they were intrigued about were things such as confession and the Virgin Mary. Incense and vestments were soon to emerge as the major differences. I was interested in their links and ways of working with other denominations and the church abroad as well as their community contacts, which we didn't seem to have. It was a two-way learning process for us all. Some even had women vicars and I voiced my beliefs in a non-threatening way and listened to their arguments. The course ran in six week blocks with six weeks in-between in which to complete projects and assignments, some written, others practical. We all did a "parish visit" when we joined in a Sunday worship at each others' church. I enjoyed this. The whole course was interesting and valuable to me. I hadn't done any real written work such as essays for years so my writing skills improved with practice. I had never been good academically, but in my case I must have improved with age, some of the work was really good. None of it was marked in the graded sense, but the tutors discussed with each individual as to how conclusions were reached and this helped to widen everyone's opinions simply by sharing thoughts and ideas. Our group got on extremely well. We were a varying lot. One was a church warden and knew a lot about the church. A couple were highly academic and already preached and led services. One was a faith healer and held a strong psychoanalytical viewpoint. Others were, like me, just starting to look to see what God might have in store for them in active service in the church. Three or four were going to continue for a third year and qualify as readers. This was not something I had in mind.

Within the family, things were settling down nicely now. I had seen little of my family since Robert's death, except June who came to visit us or rang regularly. I think both of us needed this equally as much. Our relationship had become much closer since Robert died. The brother who had stayed with me had not had a drink since the funeral and this was wonderful. Robert would have been as proud of him as I was. The rest simply got on with their lives.

My case was now looking likely to actually go to court. I had not imagined this, but my solicitor must have known. They had denied all responsibility for my injury, in fact they claimed that I had not been injured at work at all but that I had hurt myself and tried to blame a minor lifting incident for my pain, which, they said was not as bad as I was claiming. I hadn't thought of them denying the accident and it upset me to think that my colleagues didn't support me in my claim. They had visited me and brought me cards and flowers when I was in bed, so how could I have made up a story about the accident? It made no sense to me. As for the pain, I had suffered so much and had to change so much in my everyday life pattern through it that it could not possibly be worth my while to exaggerate or lie. My life was now ruled and ordered by my limitation because of the pain. I now had facet joint injections at the pain clinic at the hospital. I went in every twelve weeks as a day patient and had the injections under sedation in X-ray. Then I went to the ward to sleep off the anaesthetic and went home in the evenings. These injections give me excellent pain relief, which lasts for four to six weeks. I can do everyday things like sitting, standing and bending with little pain during this period but still I am unable to lift anything, even with the injections. I had now been seen by around ten or fifteen specialists who argued the case amongst themselves through my solicitor. My contact through phone calls, letters and visits to his office seemed to take up much of my precious spare time. At times I felt like packing it all in and just getting on with my life. My solicitor had worked so hard putting the case together and all the people on my side were so supportive that I did go on though. It became important to me to prove that I wasn't lying. If I got any compensation that would be a bonus, but the most important thing was the truth.

In September 1996 two major events in our family life took place within two weeks of each other. Marie would marry and graduate. This proved a problem to us all in that, although Ray now had a job, his wages were much less than the salary we were used to, and on top of all this the debts we had to honour, we were left financially broke. We all wanted Marie to have the best wedding we could afford. She wanted a nuptial mass in St Mary's and she would have one. The church, photographer, flowers and cars were booked and had to be paid for. Marie was still a student and she worked part-time at a newsagents in Oxford to pay for her dress and veil. Mark, her husband-to-be, contributed all he could. We all needed new outfits and the reception would be for one hundred people including family and friends. Plans for the wedding had been going on all year long and now with just a couple of weeks to go before the big day I had a letter from my solicitor. As I read it my heart was pounding. I had been offered the sum of £2,500 as a settlement figure. I waited to tell Ray before I could decide what to do. This money would be just enough to see us through the wedding and the graduation and perhaps some left over for Christmas. We knew from our previous talks with my solicitor that this was the figure they would offer me to settle out of court. If I took it we would lose nothing and they would have accepted responsibility for the accident. If I refused and took them to court we may lose. If we lost, I was on legal aid and I would not have anything to pay. After a long discussion, Ray and I decided that we would refuse the settlement payment and continue the case. I rang my solicitor and told him. He was pleased with our decision. Even if we lost, we would see this through and the truth would emerge. Not many days went by when we didn't think or talk about the case. It became the focal point of our lives for a while. I got a letter from my solicitor asking me to come to view a surveillance video that my employers had taken of me. Even though I knew I hadn't done any heavy lifting or anything, I was so worried that I couldn't sleep until we went together to see the video. They had followed me to the Post Office and to the Samaritan Centre. They even filmed me in church during a service, probably to see if I was playing the organ, which I had said I didn't do now. They also filmed me driving around our local town and going to the market in town. Here I came out with a small bag containing a pair of socks. They must have hoped I would have a bag full of heavy shopping, but they were wrong. They were going to show this video during the trial, my solicitor said. We weren't too worried about it. I breathed a deep sigh of relief as we left for home. The date of the trial was set.

She looked beautiful. Marie walked down the aisle at the church where she had been christened twenty-one years earlier. Claire was a bridesmaid and Luke an usher. The service was lovely and I only cried once, just when I saw the ring on her finger. I was proud and happy for them. They made a lovely couple. The day was perfect. I had prayed that solutions to our financial difficulties would come about and, bingo, they did. A friend paid for the limousine as a wedding gift to the couple. My brother in law took the photos and did a very good job. June gave them the cost of the honeymoon as a wedding present. Another friend catered for the reception. We costed everything right down to the after-dinner mints and she did everything on a tight budget. We had waiters and waitresses and the reception went very smoothly. Who says a wedding has to cost thousands? Money isn't everything. The celebration of their marriage was the most important thing. The service was attended by all their friends and family. We did shed a small tear as we remembered Uncle Robert who would have been so pleased for them both. Our priest and curate did a lovely service and Ray proudly read a lesson.

Two weeks later we all went to Oxford to the Sheldonian Theatre where we were proud to see Marie graduate. Ray and I were so proud and this time I did cry. She had worked so hard and had to battle with the arthritis, which plagued her from the Rheumatic Fever she had suffered as a youngster. Now on this special day we didn't think about aches and pain that she had endured so bravely, we celebrated a great achievement in her life. We, as a family, had seen so much trouble and suffering during the last year but they all disappeared as we marked two special occasions in such a short period.

In October '96 I went away on retreat for a week. A priest had told me that Mount Saint Bernard Abbey in Leicester would be a good place for me to go to have a complete escape from the world. He was right. It is a working Monastery and allowed ladies on retreat. I had considered going to Walsingham but this would be too far for me to drive. With the wedding and the graduation we were even less well off than usual. But we managed for me to go. Ray wanted me to have time on my own as much as I did. I needed time to reflect on all areas of my life. At the Monastery I was greeted by one of the monks assigned to the retreat house. I was nervous. I had never been on a week's retreat on my own, but it was a friendly and welcoming place and I soon felt at home there. During the week I went to the daily offices and joined the monks in their round of daily prayer. I attended mass each day and in between these I remained silent. This is not in any way compulsory. It was what I wanted to do. I spoke to the other guests during meal times, but then I found my own space and used the time in prayer or reflection.

I looked back on my spiritual journey and I wrote a journal. Here is part of the journal I kept during the week. I was thinking about suffering, not only mine but in general. I wrote,

"Suffering in Silence. Suffering is part of every human being's life. Christians and non-believers suffer. Suffering in silence is a well known phrase. Silence in suffering is very different. We all want to complain. It's part of our human nature. The bus is late! The soup's too hot! The washer's broken! These are just a few examples of complaints. Most of the things we complain about can be put right quite easily. But how do you cope with things which can't possibly be put right by complaining? Death, illness, poverty through war. Innocent people suffering. Man's inhumanity to Man. Debt because of unemployment or inability to earn money through illness, mental or physical. All these lead to suffering. A combination of two or more can be devastating. Complain to God! Complain to each other! Suffering in silence only leads to more suffering. If silence can be broken and suffering shared, silent people like me may find peace. Silence itself can be healing, but being afraid to speak brings pain. I pray to God that one day he will give me an answer."

Reading this now years on makes me think I have begun to find the answer. My retreat gave me a much-needed rest and the strength to face the future with fresh vigour.

Chapter 14

Christmas came and went and the New Year was quiet. All through January I worried about the court case and still prayed that they would settle out of court. But it was not to be. On Monday 24th February 1997, Ray and I drove to the court house to begin the court case. It had been four years since I had changed to this solicitor and months of work and preparation had gone into the case. My solicitor had said that they may even settle on the morning of the court date, so still I prayed silently as we walked from the car to the County Court House. I had met with my barrister the week before and we had gone through some of the details of the rules of the court. I had been shown around the actual courtroom so that I would be a little familiar and relaxed. Now we were told that we were not in the court building we should have been in, but another which was streets away. Great start! We all went to find the other building. I had chosen to wear the smart suit I had worn for Marie's graduation, I wanted to look my best. In the court foyer I saw all my expert witnesses. Also there were two of the officers from work and the woman who was lifting with me when the accident happened. Then my barrister arrived. He was robed and wearing a wig, and seeing him dressed so formally made me nervous at first, then my solicitor came and I felt more relaxed. I had grown to respect and trust him over the years since we first met. He was always strictly professional and extremely ethical and competent. He never once in all these years called me by my Christian name and I liked this. It kept a good working distance between us which I needed. Of everyone in the room, I trusted and I liked him most. Today I would need all the reassurance he could give me.

The court usher called as all into the room and we took our places. My barrister and their barrister sat at the front. They both had large files all around them, between them they had enough paperwork to fell two forests. Behind them sat my solicitor and beside him a young trainee lady solicitor whom I had met earlier in the week. Throughout the proceedings, my three would pass messages to each other. I found it fascinating and funny at the same time. They were all so serious. It was just like Crown Court on the television. Ray and I sat behind my solicitor. This was so that he could whisper to me if I needed to be told something. My friend from work, who was lifting with me on the day of the accident, sat next to Ray. She was actually in the wrong place but no one told her to move, so she didn't. At work she and I were good friends. I liked working on the same shift as her. I was still quite new as a care assistant and I asked a lot of questions. This particular friend was a good care assistant. It would be fair to say that they weren't all as caring as her. Some were reaching the end of their working lives and simply did the jobs they had to do. Others like me and the lady beside us were more conscientious in our dealings with the residents. We worked very well together.

It was all very formal. There was a lady sitting at the front facing us all who was taking recordings of the whole thing and then an usher next to her who would swear us in as we took the witness stand. Ray and I sat holding hands nervously. I wished I had never started it all as we waited for the judge to arrive. My mind was racing with negative thoughts. What if we lost? Was this really happening? I looked around and saw at least twenty people sitting there waiting to begin. All because I had complained about being sacked, knowing full well that I couldn't have done the job I was doing, even if they hadn't sacked me. It all suddenly seemed to be out of proportion and unnecessary for me and all these other people who should be at work. I saw three of the officers from work. They looked uncomfortable. I saw the video man who must have been following me. I wondered how much more film he had of me, besides the ten minutes or so that I had seen. On our left were half a dozen of our expert witnesses. They had all prepared papers on me and would now be questioned on their findings. My employer's witnesses were not there. They would come later in the week, my solicitor had told me. He had said it may go on for five days. That was how long the courtroom was booked for. This courtroom alone was costing thousands of pounds. Then as my mind wandered into panic, the judge came in through a door in the very right hand corner at the front. We all stood up, then sat down. Now I couldn't stop it. It really was going to happen. Here, just feet in front of me, was a real judge with a real wig and red cloak looking so formidable and serious. My thoughts of this being silly soon disappeared. These people weren't acting, this was going to be taken very seriously.

My barrister began by saying what I was accusing my employers of, which was failing to train me in handling and lifting, and allowing me to lift in a way which led to my injury. His version was much longer and wordy, but in a nutshell, that was what he was saying. I would hear lots of legal jargon before the end of the week. Sometimes as I sat and listened to him or their barrister, I realised just how little I knew about the law and the legal system. They talk their own language. It's a bit like church. I am familiar with clerical words and terminology. I understand their language and I am comfortable with priests. Here I was like a visitor to a wedding or baptism, simply repeating the words and in awe of the clergy, not being in daily or even regular contact with the church, feeling out of their depth. Now it was me who was out of my depth in the court setting. In time I understood, but initially fear, nervousness and insecurity were the feelings I had. I was afraid that if I lost, the judge might fine me for wasting his time or something. He even had the power to lock me up. Now I was getting paranoid. My solicitor told me, and I knew anyway, that if I lost nothing would happen. It was me who was accusing them, not the other way round. Yes I could lose, but

I was the one who was bringing a suit against my employers, not the other way round.

As I was thinking all this, my barrister was outlining the case to the court. He read my statement to them, a ten-page document relating my side of the story concerning the accident and how it had changed my life. Their barrister would question me on this later. This was why my solicitor had been so careful to help me with the wording. It was all the truth, it had to be, or I would be found out and the whole case balanced on my being believed, he had said. I didn't lie or exaggerate the accident or the after effects of it. My past, which was also being disclosed, only I knew to be true. Meanwhile my barrister was saying that I had been seen by a psychologist who came to the conclusion that I was truthful and remarkably well-balanced. Then the barrister briefly revealed details about my past, describing it as "her tragic and appalling childhood." I felt myself go red and embarrassed as people listened. It was this bit that I wanted to skip over as quickly as possible. My barrister had done this early to get it out of the way and to save me from having to say it in the witness box. He also revealed details about all my medical illnesses throughout my life. We had to tell everything as we guessed that their council wanted to claim that my pain was exaggerated. He read out loud some glowing character references from my school headmaster right through all my previous employers, up to and including a great one from my present boss Tina, one of the officers who was sitting on my right. She must have loved him! I smiled to myself. All this took him three quarters of an hour - I timed him. As he sat down I knew he was a first rate man to have on my side. He was from London and he was to travel by train every day just for my case. I thought of the first solicitor I had seen before I changed to this firm, and knew I'd made the right decision. Their barrister then stood up and said that they would prove that I was trained and that I had chosen to use an illegal lift. Even I picked up straight away that they were hedging their bets in case it didn't go they way they hoped, he added, "If this lady did hurt her back lifting, then the pain had only lasted about six months and she is now fully recovered and feigning illness to gain money from her employers".

I didn't like his manner from the moment he opened his mouth. He used the term "lady" in an almost derogatory way, and, although he was out to prove me a liar, I felt right away that he would take his task to its greatest lengths and wipe the floor with me. My barrister then opened the case for the plaintiff. I should have been called first, but he asked to hear from one of the officers first as he was not able to stay all day and could not attend the rest of the week. This man was the best of the officers. He was a hard working, hands-on carer who was well liked and respected by all the staff and the residents. He was asked about the lady I was lifting. I had said in my statement that I thought she was about seventeen stone. They said she was eleven stone. I had also said in my statement that this man had a way of lifting that was different to the one we all used, and that he had shown me how to do this lift. When asked, he said he couldn't remember ever lifting with me. He said he remembered the lady in question and that she was a particularly difficult lady to lift, and that we had a hoist to get her out of bed but this was not suitable to be used outside the bedroom. When asked, he said that he would stop people using an illegal lift if he saw them. He said he had no recollection of ever seeing me lifting. Their barrister didn't wish to cross examine him so he stood down. The judge then announced that we would end at this point and re-convene at two o'clock. Ray and I went for lunch with my friend from work and the officer who had just given his evidence. We didn't talk much about the facts of the case.

At two pm. I was called by my barrister to give my evidence. I remembered my solicitor's words as I walked up to the stand, "...the whole case will be won or lost on your credibility. If the judge believes you, you will win, if he thinks you are lying, you'll lose." Simple as that. I had no intention of lying so I had a good chance of winning. I was sworn in and took an oath on a bible. I thought that was just on the television, but it really happens. Also it amazed me that if the judge wants to ask you something you call him "Your Honour" and he can ask you anything at any time if he wants to clarify something. As I was being sworn in I saw him looking at me. He seemed big and stern but at the same time, I liked him. He smiled at me when he saw I was looking at him. He said I was to take my time and speak clearly. My heart was pounding and I felt the way I felt when I was going to make my confession in church only this time it was in public and, unlike the confessional when you are not judged, here I was clearly going to be judged on what I said. Some of the events on the day of the accident were not clear. At the time I didn't think I would ever be questioned about it so it wasn't too important. I told my version as I remembered it. If it didn't match my friend who was with me, then tough, I could only tell the truth as I remember it.

My barrister then asked me to tell the court in my own words how the accident happened. He asked me one or two things about after I got home, then he said he had no further questions. This took about ten minutes. I was more composed than I thought I would be. Inside I was shaking but outside I didn't let my nervousness show. Then their barrister stood up and began to cross-question me. He began with the osteopath, then the history of my illness from my youth up to the accident. He said my GP notes showed that I had complained little about my back pain, just visiting each month for a sick note. I had in front of me a pile of files numbered one to four. He asked me to refer to a certain page and onward where all my visits to my GP had been photocopied and all my sick notes were there. As I looked, to my horror I saw recorded the visits when I took my brothers to see my GP. He had written what we had told him and now all the experts, all my colleagues all the people sitting here in front of me, had copies. They all knew. For a moment I went into a panic and lost my place and began to fluster. I went bright red and hot. From nowhere the usher appeared with a glass of water which I thanked him for and took a sip. Then I carried on looking through the file as the barrister referred me to various points. We went through my angina and other problems which were all written down by my GP and hospital consultants. I answered truthfully and he touched on my seeing a psychotherapist. I think he wanted me to be seen as neurotic and unbalanced mentally. I stayed remarkably composed and even at one point told him that I didn't think that personal details about my brothers should be in these files and that there was never any need for my psychotherapy to have been disclosed by me to my employers or anybody else. This may not have been appropriate and could have gone against me but he made me annoyed and embarrassed showing everyone who, at the same time as me, referred to the files as we spoke. I saw the judge writing something down so I shut up and sipped my water.

At about 3 pm. we were shown the video which had been taken in June and August last year. These clearly showed me as active. I was not seen to lift or carry anything heavy or do anything strenuous. He questioned me on them until 4.30, then he said, "This lady is not in pain on the videos we have all just seen. I put it to you that she is a liar."

I told him that I was in pain but you cannot see the pain, and also that I always carried on outside as though I was not in as much pain as I was (this was not to lie), but people don't want to hear me moaning on all the time. I also said that if I kept active, it helped me to cope better with the pain. I agreed that I didn't look like a lady in pain on the video, but I am. I looked at the judge, then at the barrister and said, "I am in pain right now, but you can't see how much my back is hurting." I had been standing for nearly three hours now and my back was killing me but even here, I tried to let it not show. He then started to ask me about my pain injections at the hospital. At this point the judge stopped him and said we would re-convene in the morning at 10 a.m. He turned to me and said, "You are still under oath and still in the stand, therefore you must not discuss the case with anyone, not even your solicitor. Do you understand?"

I replied, "Yes your Honour,"

Then he said to the barristers, "I wish to see you both in my chambers."

A Saint I Ain't

Then the usher said, "All rise," and the judge went out. We all left the courtroom.

It felt strange and uncomfortable not being able to speak to my solicitor. I wanted to ask him what he thought. Did I do wrong with my little outburst? Was he annoyed with me? We had strayed a lot from my statement and sometimes I wasn't sure what he would want me to say. Some of their barristers questions were very tricky. Oh well. I had done what I had done and there was no going back now.

In the car on the way home we did talk about the day, of course. I felt numbed. The barrister had questioned me heavily. I asked him how I had come across and Ray said I had done well. Neither of us could decide if I had said too much or not enough. Ray was not as optimistic as I was. He said he thought we might lose. Their barrister was tough, mine was more gentle, as he would be because he was on my side. I kept on saying all the way home, "I told the truth, that's all that matters."

I didn't sleep all that night. My head was so full of worries and fears. I could hear their barrister saying, "You are a liar, you are not a lady in pain. The lady in the video is not in pain." Then I started to think that if I lost the case and I was proved to be a liar, would my solicitor believe me? Would there be reports in the newspapers saying, "Director of the Samaritans found guilty of lying." What about all my friends who knew about the case? How would I tell them if I lost? How would the judge word it if I was found guilty? Should I have been limping more to show them that I was in pain? But I didn't usually limp. The injections gave me a lot of freedom now. There was a time when I used a walking stick, I still had it, but if I used it tomorrow in court, they would know I didn't need it at the moment.

The next day on the way to court we were more subdued than the previous day. I was much more nervous now. I thought about their barrister. He had used a fairly threatening approach yesterday, today he might be worse. I could see him now, clutching on to the lapels on his gown as he questioned me, talking in a condescending manner and adding suggestive comments to my replies and insinuating that all I said was a lie.

"I suggest to you that this is not true," he had said so many times when he questioned my accusation that I had never been given any lifting training. I had been told by my bosses to miss the handling and lifting session during the induction so I and the other kitchen staff could see to the orders coming in and sort out the kitchen. How was I to know that this would be questioned so many years later, with his reply being, "how convenient."

When we got to the court we found we had been moved to the new court building where I had been shown round a week before. This was better. It was more open and modern than the other and there was a cafe where we could get a drink. I saw my solicitor who, after asking how I was, reminded me that we couldn't speak about the case as I was still under oath. He took Ray into an interview room and I went over to my friend who I was lifting with at the time of the accident. She had since left Oakdale and was now living and working in Lincolnshire. She told me that she didn't get home until ten o'clock the previous night and that she had to be on the 6.30 am train this morning to be here for ten. We joked about overtime. I hoped she would be heard today so that she didn't have to come back the following day.

At 10 am. we were called into the courtroom. As the judge came in we all stood, then sat down, all except me. I went to the witness stand and was reminded by the judge that I was still under oath. Their barrister picked up where he had left off, and began to ask about my facet joint injections. As time went on he fired questions at me, referring me to the large files in front of me. My mouth was dry and I kept losing my place. He was impatient with me and got louder and angrier, quicker than yesterday. I knew he was trying to unnerve me and I tried not to show how he was upsetting me. The usher had provided me with water to begin with and this helped. He repeatedly called me a liar and this got to me, but I kept as calm as I could. This was difficult because I knew this was a real trial. I was accusing my employers of serious neglect. When I originally told my solicitor about the accident, I

A Saint I Ain't

had described how I was lifting the lady. I said, "I had my right arm under her armpit and my partner had her arm under the lady's other arm pit. We lifted and half turned her, when she slipped and fell and pulled me over with her. My partner let go and I took her full weight alone."

I was not then aware when I told him this that I was using a lift banned by lifting experts. Now they had to admit that this banned lift is still being used in all homes owned by my employers. I had inadvertently let the cat out of the bag. They would go to any lengths to call me a liar. The responsibility for all this lay squarely on me now that I had started it. I was frightened that if I won, there could be jobs at stake for some employees. How would I live with this?

I remained on the stand for an hour and a half and when he had finished with me, the judge asked me some questions. He had shown himself to be discerning as well as sharp at times, especially with their barrister. He seemed to question their barrister on his handling of their side of the case more than he did mine. When he spoke to me the judge was polite and kind. At times he stopped everything and went out into his chamber to look in private at certain points raised by one thing or another. I sort of trusted that he was going to be fair. I was less nervous of him than I was of their barrister (he wouldn't really lock me up!). When the judge had finished questioning me, I was told that I may stand down. I went back to sit beside Ray. He shook my hand in a reassuring way. I was hot and flustered, dry-mouthed and shaking like a leaf. I was glad it was over for me, now I would sit and listen to the rest.

My lifting partner was the next to be called. I was glad it was her, she wanted to be off at lunch time. My barrister asked her if she remembered the accident and she said she didn't. Then he asked her about the lifting method she used while working at the home. She said she had left the area years ago and she couldn't remember. He had no further questions and their barrister had none so she stood down. I was a little surprised and a little hurt at the way she disclaimed almost any knowledge of me and our working together, but in hindsight I realised that it had to be this way. She couldn't admit that she was lifting illegally so she conveniently forgot. It actually did my case a favour I suppose. If she had said she had never used that lift, then it would have been difficult for us. We would have to prove she did. Anyway she was finished with now. Then my barrister called our psychologist. He gave a long and detailed psychological profile on me and the judge asked him lots of questions. He explained that because of my childhood, I had developed a way of coping with stress, which has a long medical title. The top and bottom of it is that despite my history of abuse, I was well-balanced psychologically and showed little or no sign of depression. He believed that I was in a long term chronic condition which came and went depending on what I did. He said that I had developed a way of coping with stress and pain, which I had had to do all my life. It was all rather complicated but he explained it well enough at the time for us all to understand.

Their barrister then made out that I was making everything up to gain attention. The psychologist said that this was not true, after which he stood down. Then their psychiatrist was called. I had seen him twice and his reports were almost the same as my psychologist. Now on the witness stand he said he agreed with everything the last witness had said and that in his opinion, I "presented to him as a very honest lady whose sad background was true and that I had coped very well." He then said to the judge, "She is not a liar."

I felt giddy inside as I listened. There was no point in their barrister cross-questioning him as he may as well have been on my side. He stood down. The judge said we would break for lunch and he went out. I was very excited now. I felt confident that we were doing well and I couldn't wait to speak to my solicitor. As I turned to get up I saw Ray rush from the room with my solicitor and the lady who did the home care profile following him. I hadn't noticed in my highly excited state that Ray had become very upset. I saw the last two witnesses as supportive, but

Ray had felt for me and he said he thought they were "assassinating my character". As my solicitor and the lady consoled him I stood back and thought for a moment. Poor Ray. He had to listen to all this being said about me. I hadn't thought until this was happening that he was not nearly as well prepared as I was. I had knowledge of what they were going to say. I had been through two full case conferences with all my team of witnesses, he hadn't. I had met regularly with my solicitor who had guided me all the way. It was me who had been given all the tests, medicals, interviews, read all the reports. Most importantly, they were talking about me and I knew that all the words in the world couldn't hurt me in the end. I was so sorry for Ray but I daren't go to him or I would breakdown with him. I swallowed a big lump in my throat and soon we went to the cafe for a cup of tea and some lunch. We spoke quietly and calmly. They would not get to us, we agreed, we would remain strong. We were right to do what we were doing. They were the sad ones who had resorted to trying to discredit me, but they were failing. They were not going to win by using underhand tactics and that was all this was, they were in a corner and the only way out was to fight dirty. They couldn't win on the truth so they had tried to get me to back out by hitting me where it hurt most, my private life, but they had just failed.

After lunch we resumed in court. The boss of the home was called. She was asked about the induction course and my training but she said she remembered nothing. She said she knew nothing about any accident. She was asked how certain documents regarding my training were filled in after the accident. The court was shown signed documents which said I attended training sessions after I had the accident. I was never at work again, let alone on training days! She said she had never seen me lifting. As I listened I knew she had dropped herself right in it. I felt even more optimistic. Then Ray was called by my barrister. Ray told how on the day of the accident, not long after I came home, he had been rung by an officer to see if I could work an extra shift.

He had told her about the accident and that we were waiting for the doctor to ring back. He said the next day he rang work and told them that the locum had said I had a slipped disc and I would be off work for at least a month. Then their barrister cross-questioned him, saying that he had called, but had made no reference to an accident at work. He said that Ray had told them I had a "bad back", and not that I had hurt it at work. Ray denied this, saying that as a shift manager at work, he himself knew that onus of reporting accidents fell on the shift manager and that once he told them, they should have filled in the accident report book. The barrister said, "But there was no accident to report, was there?" He went on, "I put it to you that you are making this up to support your wife!" Ray denied this.

He said he had no further questions, then he turned and stared at me as he had done most of the afternoon, I'd noticed. He would look at me when he thought no one could see and stare in a strange, almost challenging manner, trying to, and indeed succeeding in making me feel uncomfortable. I never told anyone, but Ray saw as well. I really didn't like this man.

At this point the judge said he had some questions for Ray. He began by saying that this case had brought to light some very difficult areas in my private life. He asked Ray how he felt about this. I was worried as I waited for Ray to answer. It had only been an hour or so since he had been upset at my past, and its resulting ongoing problems, being disclosed and analysed in public. I hoped he wouldn't be too sensitive and not be able to answer him. Ray told the judge that talking about it together had been a good thing for us both. The judge asked him when he first learned about my childhood and Ray said, "After her mother's death." The judge thanked him and said he could leave the witness stand.

As Ray came back to sit beside me I wished we could both leave and go home now. Let them all carry on without us, I thought. Ray took hold of my hand again and we both smiled a nervous but reassuring smile to each other. It was too late to stop it now, we had done all we could, telling the truth was all we had to do. Now it was up to my experts to finish giving reports.

A Saint I Ain't

The doctor from the pain clinic was next. He explained the treatment I had received since 1995. He concluded that this treatment would continue as long as he felt it necessary. He said that he had many patients who had long term pain which, like mine, was managed with physiotherapy, tablets to relieve the inflammation around the damaged area, injections as a day patient and also a programme from a psychologist to help with the psychological damage (which is common to many patients in long term chronic pain). Added to this, he said that the strain of feelings of rejection from losing my job and not being able to look after my house and family as I did before the accident, meant that I would have to continue to come to terms with many losses. As to the psychological unbalance, which their barrister said I was suffering from, he said, "I agree with the two psychotherapist's reports which I have read. This lady, apart from not pacing herself as she should, is remarkably well adjusted taking into account her background, and although she will never be "cured" of past damage, her life can be made easier, especially with further psychotherapy."

Then their barrister stood up and exclaimed loudly, "The lady on the video is not in pain!" The doctor replied calmly, that physical pain cannot be measured and no one can see how much pain another person is in. People choose to show pain as and how they will.

"So," the barrister shouted, "she turns the pain of and off as she wishes, that is what is termed attention seeking, is it not?"

The doctor said that in his opinion I was not attention seeking in any way, but that the pain was real and I coped with it the best I could so as to get on with my daily life. The judge asked him some questions about the pain injections and long term pain management and then he left the stand. Then the lifting and handling expert was called and he said that the injury I had was consistent with the description of the accident, taking into consideration the weight of the lady and the method of lifting I was using. My barrister stood and said, "This then concludes the witnesses for the plaintiff, your honour." He would give a closing address at the end of the case when the judge had heard the case for the defendants.

The judge left the room after saying that we would reconvene in the morning at 10 am. He added, "I want to have heard all other witnesses by tomorrow lunch time so that I can have all Wednesday afternoon to consider, and I will give my conclusion on Thursday."

Chapter 15

My barrister and solicitor were very happy with the way it was all going. Their barrister was getting more and more anxious and at times, rude. But the judge kept him in order. I definitely felt that we had a strong case. I didn't care about the financial outcome. My solicitor said he thought we wouldn't be awarded wages for life, especially as I was gaining pain relief from treatment. I really didn't care. I knew now that the courtroom had cost forty thousand pounds for the five days it was booked for. The legal aid board would pay everything if I lost, and if I won, my employer's insurance would have to pay. They would also have to pay my solicitors fees, barrister and witness costs, as well as some personal costs incurred by me since the accident, including five years' prescription costs, the cost of a new orthopaedic bed we had bought to help my pain at night. There were also alterations in my home including bath rails, an eye level oven as I could no longer use my oven, a high seat chair I had bought. All these and many more little things all add up. Then there was five years loss of wages, costs of travel and phone calls to his office and to attend dozens of medical and legal

A Saint I Ain't

appointments I have been to over the last few years, and then an amount for pain and suffering, my solicitor had said.

On Wednesday at 10 am. we were called by the usher back into court. It now seemed like a very long time since Monday morning when it all began. As a family we talked all the time about the case, often into the night. It was like a living nightmare. I couldn't take in what was happening. One minute I felt positive, the next I didn't. I was at the mercy of the judge who, I felt, seemed to believe me. During the times when the judge went out of the courtroom and into his chambers to consider something, we went into the corridor.

I could smell the court house all the time, even in bed after a long hot bath, the distinctive smell and feel remained. There in the corridors I saw men and women, old and young, some with babies in prams. Some would be witnesses, others accused of one thing or another. Barristers in wigs and gowns greeted each other politely. Policemen did their daily jobs. A court is a strange place to be in. Ray and I had never been in a court before. For us we could be happy with the knowledge that, win or lose, we were not in any trouble. But looking at the worried expressions on the faces of some of the people in the corridors and the cafe, not all were as fortunate as we were. I sometimes felt like a fraud. They were not as lucky as me. I had a great supporting team of medical and legal experts speaking for me, and the fullest support of family and friends. No matter how it went, win or lose, I could, and would, walk out and get back to my everyday life. In this building it was as if we were confined within these walls, searched as we entered each day, then encapsulated in a strange world of legal, moral and ethical questions and theories. People were looking at my behaviour and conduct, potentially to clear my blotted character, blackened only to save the face of my employers. Now the very people I had worked with and for were breaking the conventional rules of behaviour by lying; trying to prove that the accident had not happened while I was working for them, by using any means whatsoever to discredit me. They could not get away with it, surely? Well today we would know. We could do no more than to sit and listen to what their witnesses and legal team had to say. Today it would be over.

The courtroom was much emptier now. The only witnesses present were two of the officers from the home and an employment consultant. I spoke briefly to my barrister and my solicitor who were both very optimistic of a win. Then we all stood as the judge came in and their barrister called the first witness. The other two officers who had been called by my barrister were in fact witnesses for my employers but whose evidence was needed to back up my claims. Today these two were called simply to prove that I was lying and so they were called by their barrister, not mine. First to be called was the lady who had rung on the day of my accident to ask me to work an extra shift. The barrister asked her about the phone contact with Ray. She said she couldn't remember if he called her or if she called him. This was silly I thought as I listened. She rang to speak to me to ask me if I would work an extra shift, so of course she rang us. She said that she remembered he said I couldn't do the extra shift because I had a bad back, but he made no mention as to any accident, she said. The barrister thanked her then mine stood up and repeated what she had said, "Her husband made no mention of the accident," and she said that was correct. He said, "What if he had mentioned it, would she have put it in the accident report book?" She said yes, she would. He asked her if all calls were logged. She said yes. Then she stood down. That went well, I thought. Then the officer who received Ray's call on the Saturday after I had been seen by the locum was called to the stand. Their barrister asked her if she remembered Ray's call and she said yes she did. She remembered he had said that I had been seen by a doctor who said I had a slipped disc and would have to be off work for a while. She said that Ray made no mention of how I had hurt my back. Then my barrister stood up and again, repeated what she had just said adding, "Did you think it strange that he didn't say what she had done to hurt her back?" She said she really couldn't remember, it was a long time ago. He asked if anyone at the home knew how I had hurt my back. She replied that she knew some staff had visited me at home when I was first off sick, but she knew nothing about an accident. Then she stood down. Once again I felt sad. Then an employment consultant whom I had never met was called and briefly said that I could find non-physical clerical work easily even with a bad back. My barrister argued the point. The case for the defence had been short and in my opinion, so weak that even I was embarrassed at their arguments.

My barrister gave an excellent concluding address, outlining so many flaws and blatantly obvious attempts to deny all knowledge of the accident. Even when it was pointed out to the court that many adaptations to lifting this particular lady including talks and demonstrations, all documented after Jan 1991, he believed it to be too much of a coincidence. He commented about the lifting method which I said I was using. Finally he outlined that my personal credibility and character was proved to be that of an honest person who was not a malingerer, with nothing to gain from lying. He pointed out that I was receiving treatment from a highly respected consultant who believed I would benefit from his treatment and was willing to continue it as a long as necessary. A lady who still in fact, even while in pain, continuing her eleven year long commendable charity work which she is able to do because of the flexibility and non-physical nature of the work. Also having the fullest continued support of her family and the legal and medical team during all the years of this injury, who all believe what she says is true. He ended by saying that my employers were liable for all the costs of the case, compensation of at least five years loss of wages, plus expenses for the pain and suffering as a result of the accident.

Then their barrister stood up and said that the accident did not happen as I said because I failed to report it. I had a history of long term unexplained angina which he thought I was making up. I was psychologically unbalanced and making it all up to gain compensation from my employers.

That was it, it was all over. The judge started to ask about hourly rates of pay I was on when I was working. He said he wouldn't consider wages forever, though. He said he would have to get his calculator out and he would reconvene at 10.30 in the morning to give his conclusion.

We knew now we had won. I felt elated. Their barrister and mine were arranging a meeting and my solicitor congratulated us. It was still low key and formal at this stage for them. Ray and I were so giddy in the car all the way home. I couldn't believe we had done it. It was never going to be a straightforward case, my solicitor had repeatedly told me, and it wasn't. Even my barrister was never seen to be over confident. But we had won. The truth counts for something. At home I felt numb. I cried a lot, more with relief than happiness. We told only the children, one of my deputies and my parish priest. The rest would find out the next day. I still didn't sleep that night. I thought about all the things that I had been made to disclose and which were now common knowledge to so many people.

At 10.30 in court on Thursday morning there was just Ray and me, my barrister, solicitor and the young lady trainee who had assisted them, their barrister and his assistant, plus usher and recorder of course. The judge came in and began his summing up. He began by saying that he believed all the Ray and I had said and that my employers were fully liable because they failed to train me, but allowed me to lift in a manner which proved to cause me an injury. He awarded me damages and compensation and said that my employers were to pay all the costs incurred during the five years of the case. In all it cost my employers over £100,000. If they had settled out of court that sum would have been less then half. When I had repaid, as I was legally bound to do, my five years of invalidity (which came to more than £17,000), my legal fees, all my witnesses who did reports and medicals in full, and the £40,000 for the court for the week, I received quite a few thousands for myself.

The following week I arrived in Walsingham for a well-earned four-day break. The weather was beautiful, sharp and spring-like as it was now early March. It was Saturday afternoon and the village was quite empty. I made my first visit to the Holy House and lit a candle, thanking God for a safe journey and praying that now I could begin to rebuild my life again, knowing that the trial was over and I had won. Every day since the accident, the pain was a constant reminder. I walked slowly to my car, took out my small bag containing just enough clothes for my few days of quiet, and the paper and pens which I was going to use to write down the account of the trial. I had planned to do this whether I had won or lost the case. As it happened, it would have a happy ending. It will never however be erased from my memory completely. The things I heard and felt during this week would remain with me forever. I have always tried to write down the things which bother me. For me it is a therapeutic thing to do. I include facts, thoughts and feelings around certain situations which I have found myself troubled by, but which I cannot express verbally. Once they are on paper I can do with them what I want. Sometimes I show someone. Other times I burn it, or I keep it safe somewhere and perhaps re-read it later.

I went to see the room I was staying in and, after unpacking, I went back to the shrine and spent some quiet time in the grounds. Later in church I released the tears which I had held for so long. I wept loudly and couldn't stop. I spoke to no one, words were not needed to be said or heard. God was the only witness I needed or wanted. In my room after supper I began my writing. The next day I wrote in the morning, then after lunch I took the car and went to a bird sanctuary on the coast. Listening to the sea and feeling the wonderful sharp salty sea air on my face, cold as ice, yet invigorating, I watched the birds fly freely as they called to one another in flight. Once again my tears flowed in sheer relief that I too was now free. My case now over I didn't have to worry any more. But I felt now, in having to release things which up until then only I knew and had been forced to hold on to, I was now a freer person in other ways too. My past was slowly being opened and bit by bit dealt with, each time in a new and unplanned way.

The rest of my retreat, in-between writing, was spent eating, sleeping, praying, or driving to the coast to get fresh air. All these were things which I had to forfeit, willingly or unwillingly, in the weeks and days running up to and throughout the trial. During the trial I felt strangely detached from everything and everyone from which I usually found comfort. During my stay in this Holy place, or on the beach alone, I found space and privacy to cry. Releasing my built up tears was important to me at this time. Every day I wept either for myself or for others who had been at the forefront of my thoughts recently. I needed to do this so that when I got home, I could pick up my pattern of daily routine once more. Crying and allowing myself to show my true feelings were not as a rule part of this routine. For the first time in many years, mainly since Ray left the steel works, we had extra money to spend on the house and to treat ourselves as a family. My compensation money would be used to benefit us all. The accident had affected all the family, so they all deserved a share. Together we talked about the things we would do with the money. It was to go on the house as well as for personal things. I thought back to the closing address my barrister had given, which included things which I have needed as a result of the accident, and things which I could no longer do. As the case drew near to completion, all the hard facts of the accident and incidents that were raised around my tainted background. My solicitor quite rightly suggested that they would use this to discredit my character, and we were prepared.

There was left one other area which needed to be brought out at trial. This was the effect that the accident had on my life afterwards and how I coped. I went to his office one day to begin to put together a brief account of the changes I had to make. This was to take many weeks altogether and when it was completed,

A Saint I Ain't

even I was surprised at the amount of changes I had made. It was obvious that their barrister would say that they were exaggerated, but if anything, we left a lot out. There was my motor bike and the organ, which I had got rid of in a moment of frustration. But there was so much more I couldn't do now. I used to enjoy cooking and baking. Now I only cooked what we needed, when I was able to cook. Baking for pleasure was never to be enjoyed again. Mixing by hand is still impossible - even the Yorkshire pudding on a Sunday is mixed by Ray or Luke. Cake decorating, a skill I learned from Ray's mum, now I couldn't do. Crouching over a cake to fill in small details in icing is too painful. Everyday baking is out too. Rolling out pastry or kneading bread or mixing stiff batters makes the pain increase, so I couldn't do these any more. These can, and are replaced with shop bought pies, pasties and cakes, but they aren't as good as home made, I told my solicitor. The garden was now a mass of tangled weeds in summer and mud in the winter. Ray and I used to do the garden together before the accident. Now five years on it had deteriorated to such a state that it was an embarrassment. Ray hadn't the time any more. When he finished work, there were often things in the house which he needed to do because of the limitations my pain imposed. We used to love our garden. I could keep the grass cut if he was working. One of us, or both of us, would cut the hedges and weed flower beds. We used to grow our own veg. The roses in the front and at the side of the house were especially beautiful. I kept a rose bowl in the lounge for most of the year. The smell of them filled the room. Large deep purple irises grew under the window, enough for me to cut for the house and often some left over which went towards decorating the church. Now all I could see from my window front and back were weeds, overgrown grass and garden tools left to rust by the broken-down garden fence. I was finding it more and more difficult to get up the garden path, let alone dig it. The shed had a hole in the roof and the greenhouse was a mass of thistles where tomatoes and even a grape vine once flourished. New bedding plants waited there to be planted out. Now it was filled with dirty plant pots and containers housing spiders and slugs. When I looked out in summer, it made me very sad to see such a lovely garden had gone. It gave me a lump in my throat as I told the solicitor.

The interior of the house was also showing signs of neglect. I have never put housework before the family or relaxation, but we had a tidy, comfortable house once. Now it needed decorating. Ray and I did all our own painting and decorating. Ray's DIY skills with me as his apprentice made house maintenance easy and enjoyable. Not only time, but I suppose the pleasure of doing it together which was now gone, led Ray to put off the household maintenance work until it was desperate. I couldn't do the heavy jobs any more. The windows used to get done regularly. Now I pestered Ray to do them. The curtains were left. Getting them down was never a problem. I could ask Ray or one of the children and they would get them down for me to pop in the washer. Getting them back up was a nightmare. Sometimes it took me days to get someone to put them up. "Oh, I will later mum," or "I'll do them after tea love." I would sit and stew angrily as they left them. The curtains then got left till the following day so as to avoid another argument. Eventually they got done. All women will know the feeling, I told my solicitor, and we both laughed. But it isn't funny - arguing and sulking over windows and curtains, how sad.

I suppose one thing money can't make up for is the loss of choice. Before I was in constant pain I could choose how to spend my spare time. My working hours had increased since I went on to care. This didn't bother me. We still went on holiday as a family and the camping holidays we used to enjoy would have to go. But now I found that the days dragged. I never had time to think about spare time when I was working. Some of the extra time I did have was taken up with the Samaritans or church, so on the whole my life had a fairly steady pattern to it. For the first year or so after the accident my physical ability was very restricted. Then my body adjusted to the damage the injury had caused. There must have come a time when it, my body, found its own equilibrium. It sort of balanced out. My mind and my body had to come to terms with the realisation that this was the way it was to be. I still had conflicting thoughts. I would go so long, contented with the limits the accident had placed on me, then I would go through periods of resentment that I couldn't do the things I wanted to do. Not the things I used to do. Accepting that I could no longer do the housework and social activities as before came to be accepted more easily than the frustration of not being able to do small things right now, when I wanted to do them, not when other people could do them for me or with me. This was in addition to being limited in my choices in future. It was all confusing and made me angry and sad at the same time. So we would use the money to ease life for all of us.

The first thing I did was to get quotes from gardeners. I wanted the back garden levelled so that I could sit in it in the summer. Then we decided that we would have double-glazing to help secure the house inside and out for the future. With the loss of Ray's salary and my wages stopping we thought we would never afford this. We replaced much of our carpets and had every room in the house redecorated. This, and the new lounge suite and other small items of furniture throughout the house including new nets up to the windows, would make life much more comfortable for all of us.

The gardeners worked throughout spring and by summer we had a lovely landscaped garden. We planned it to be as easy to maintain as possible. Ray's free time was still limited to weekends and I didn't want him weeding and pruning the garden on his days off. The lawns we had were bordered with bark chippings and a trough of gravel on which was placed barrels to hold plants. This was all at a high level so that I could tend them as well. The steps to the lower and upper level had hand rails to assist me. On the bottom we had a fish pond and now I sit and watch the fish in the afternoon.

One thing I wanted to give the children was driving lessons. These are a luxury which young people want and often can't afford. It means though that in the future, holding a driving licence could help them get a job and cut travelling costs to work for them. It also holds a freedom of its own which can't be measured. We all had a small sum which we had to spend on ourselves. Times had been hard for us all lately and, although we never exactly starved, we did reach a stage where making ends meet and living on Ray's income alone was very difficult. Some luxuries which we had given up were now re-introduced into daily life. Money could never make up for the pain and suffering I had lived through over the last five years, but it could indeed make life more bearable now.

The following year Ray and I would reach our twenty-fifth wedding anniversary. We had so much to be thankful for. We would have to think of a special way to celebrate. After months of debates, discussions and changing of minds, we came up with the perfect answer. We booked and paid for a ten-day holiday touring Italy. The compensation money slowly dwindled. But we all agreed that the changes in our circumstances, brought about as a direct result of my injury, were made easier without the worry of bills and debts. The answer for us as a family was to have a big spending splash, then tighten our belts again and continue with our life. We have never had a large amount of cash like this to do with as we wanted, so I said we would do everything all at once, then get back to normal, and we did. The court case and everything around it began slowly to be a distant memory.

Chapter 16

As part of the pastoral workers course, we all had to complete a Summer Placement. This involved spending a week living in a religious community. We had three to choose from. I chose to spend a week staying at a convent in Whitby. This experience of living, if only for a week, within a religious order, keeping their rule of prayer, scriptural study and a time devoted to leisure, which I found was almost what I had been doing all my life without even realising it. It showed me that it is possible to do this in the form which I already had, within the structure of a marriage. The vows the nuns make of chastity and obedience to God, I had been keeping within the vows of marriage. During this week I came to realise that having a husband and children made me no less committed to God than these devoted ladies who live in a family-like situation. I realised that I too was fulfilling my obligation to God in the way that He must have chosen for me. God uses each one of us in our own unique way. I felt that God wanted me to work as part of the outside community, not just the church. In the parish I was putting into practice the things I had learned during the course. I began to visit those who had recently been bereaved. I attended some of the funerals and then went to see how some of the close relatives were coping with the loss of a loved one. It sounds depressing, but it wasn't. It was very rewarding for me and gave them an opportunity to talk to someone outside their family. We did sometimes touch on God or the church, but this was not primarily the reason for the visit. It is to let the bereaved speak about their loss.

This kind of visiting was also something that I could do even with the limits my pain placed on me. I knew that if I was working at a paid job, my employer would expect me to be available for regular hours. I could never say from day to day how much pain I would be in and if I needed to stay in all day, I could. I did as much as I could, then rested. I also enjoyed passing on some of the things I gained from the course to my fellow Christians in church. I still get excited when I find something new about God, the church or faith and I want to share this with others. Doing the course has helped me to express myself in a new and clearer way I think.

Today, my active church life also helps to take my mind off my back pain and my restricted future. At times I do find I increase my pain unnecessarily, so I stop myself and slow down. I'm still not good at pacing myself and I still don't show any outward signs that I am in pain. This is not to be seen as a martyr - *a saint I ain't* - as my family and spiritual directors and priests would gladly verify. But I need to carry on unseen as long as I can, and I will not let my friends and neighbours see how much pain I am in. Silly really as I know. I would get heaps of care and sympathy, but I really don't want it, thank you.

I have taken up swimming for exercise and eat a healthy diet to keep the weight down which in turn helps my back. I still have regular pain injections and see all the people at the pain clinic who help me to keep a good balance on medical and psychological aspects of pain management. I also find that my TENS machine helps me when I need an extra boost of pain relief. I bought this expensive piece of equipment as part of my treat from my share of the money. It runs on batteries. I attach two large pads on my spine where the pain is, and the machine passes electrical impulses through to the site. This doesn't take the pain away, but it masks it, so that my mind concentrates on the impulses, not the pain. It takes practice to get the best out of it and at times I thought I had wasted my money. Now I do find it a great relief and often wear it and no one ever knows. I wear it to the Samaritans when I am on duty and to church during the services and I do find it useful when I am in the supermarket. Until you have a bad back like me you don't realise just how many miles you walk simply doing the shopping at the supermarket.

On 19th July we set off for our holiday of a lifetime. Neither of us had been abroad on holiday before so it was a new adventure for us both. We settled on Italy because it has a great variety of religious and historical places which interested us both. Ray had always wanted to see Rome and the Catacombs and I had dreamed of seeing the Basilica of St Francis, my favourite saint, in Assisi. The holiday we chose began with the first night in Paris, then the next day, on through the French Alps and the Mont Blanc Tunnel into Italy. On to Lake Como, then on 22nd July we spent a romantic day (along with thirty odd others on the same holiday) in Florence. As she knew it was our twenty-fifth wedding anniversary, the tour guide arranged with the hotel for champagne and a cake for us as a surprise. Everyone signed a card which we would keep to hold the memory. We spent overnight stops in good hotels throughout Italy. We visited Florence, Sienna and Assisi, Rome and Venice. Such sights sounds and smells we will never forget. The many fields of sunflowers, the vineyards and lakes. We soaked up the grandeur of the art, history and religious buildings of the largest and most beautiful cities and towns Italy had to offer. Monuments from the beginning of time and main streets of the towns and cities crammed full of life today with all its good and its bad aspects. We will never forget our twenty-fifth wedding present to ourselves. The last night we spent back in Paris before the return ferry back to Dover and home. I was glad we had taken a video camera. At first I didn't want it, now I am very glad we did, I watch it if I feel down.

My holiday gave me a wonderful view of how people in other countries live and work. Back at home we soon got back to real life. All our three children have jobs now and, although I say they are independent young adults now, they all still do call on Mum at the drop of a hat to pluck them out of some minor disaster or other, but that's what Mums are for. Marie, now twenty-five and two years married, visits often for a cuppa and a moan, which I don't mind as she listens to my moans too. She now has a full time job working for the British Temperance League helping to promote an alcohol and drug free lifestyle for young people and adults alike. She of all people has seen the effect alcohol abuse has on families. Luke who's twenty-three spends more time here than he does in his flat - well why not, the foods cheaper here, the phone's free and the washing powder box is bottomless so he's not daft! Claire, the baby of the family at eighteen, is still happily at home with me and her dad and she too makes the most of the free phone, the full fridge, and the never ending stream of hot water for the long hot baths which tie up the bathroom for hours. Ray is working hard and we have no financial worries at the moment, but that won't last forever. He still wants a dog to replace Trudy our lovely American Cocker Spaniel who sadly died so young. But at the moment, the fish in the garden are keeping him occupied. His hair is now a distinguished grey colour, not surprising with all he had to put up with living with me.

That leaves me. Well, as always, I'm the eternal optimist, as confident and cheerful as old Mr Micawber. My innocent, simple almost childlike actions amuse or irritate, please or displease those who have to bear them. When things go wrong, I have an almost instant urge to say, "Oh well, it could have been worse." What you see is what you get with me. I speak the truth, which is usually not what the man in the street wants to hear, but that's the way I am.

My term of office as Director came to an end. During those three long and rarely quiet years I slowly but surely regained all my self-esteem. I took over as The Director at the AGM in 1995, a rather shy and timid person. I knew I had the ability to do the job ahead of me, but the role of director unfolds, as it were, as time goes on. I did have a plan to work to, and a team of people who supported me locally and nationally, but I still never knew from one week to another what might be in store. Flexibility and being able to jump in with both feet has a part to play, as has accepting that decisions, once made, have to be seen through. Only I knew that I had never had such responsibility placed upon me in my life before. All my working life I had taken orders from superiors. I didn't have the academic qualifications which many of my fellow Samaritans had. Up to the night of this AGM I had never chaired a meeting of such a large number of people, all looking to me suddenly as the "font of all knowledge" - the boss, the one in charge. Soon I would be giving press statements, posing for photos in the local papers, and giving talks live on the radio. I would be representing a highly respected and large charity.

One evening very soon after I had taken over as director I was to attend a dinner where I would receive a large cheque from a group of powerful local dignitaries. Doctors and consultants, church leaders and company directors, business men, politicians and lawyers. I was very nervous as I got ready at home. "You'll be fine," Ray said reassuringly. I drove to the exclusive restaurant where the dinner and presentation, plus a photo of course, was to be. I was waved by the doorman into my allotted car park space. My little red panda looked rather small alongside the large posh cars in the car park. Never mind, I thought, at least mines paid for, these will be mostly company cars. I didn't feel inferior, a little out of my depth perhaps and very nervous, but subordinate never. My assertiveness came as I was shown into the entrance hall in the hotel. I was greeted by a very friendly man who asked what I would like to drink. I accepted and asked for a white wine. I looked into the dining room where people were gathering. It had been arranged that the newspaper photographer would take the photo before the dinner, then get off. As a waitress took my coat, he arrived and we went into the garden at the back with the president of the club who had donated a large sum to support our work. Photo over, I was shown into the dining room. To my horror, it was only then that I realised I was the only woman in a room of thirty or forty men, except of course, the waitresses. I was shown to the top table and felt the room relax into respectful silence as they all watched us take our place. This must rate as the most nerve-racking first five minutes in any evening before or since. I felt so alone and vulnerable in the male enclave. Then as the dinner began, I settled down and relaxed to enjoy the meal. After this was the presentation. When I had received my cheque, I would leave and they would continue the formal business. The president nodded for me to prepare myself then, after ringing a bell to ask for silence, he stood and introduced me, saying that I already had the cheque in my bag and that I wished to say a few words before going off to spend it. They all laughed which helped to ease my nervousness. As I tried to stand, my legs went to jelly and my mouth dried up. I wished now that I had written something down, but I had thought, as I only had to say thank you and go, I would improvise. Not a good idea - my mind went blank. Then as I opened my mouth to speak, the room deathly silent, a phone rang loudly in the foyer. A voice from my audience, I rather suspect in an attempt to abate my nervousness with humour said, "Its for you Mary." I laughed and, looking to the foyer said, "Tell them I'm not on duty tonight, I'm out to dinner." They all laughed and I did my thank you speech very well. Saved by the phone.

There were many more receptions, dinners, buffets and lunches in the three years ahead. I met with the workers from the local women's refuge, the mayor and mayoress, our local MP and many others from neighbouring agencies both government-run or volunteer-run like ours. I chaired dozens of meetings and eventually became, if I do say so myself, quite a confident, lively and outspoken director over the months and years to come. I was well liked and easy to approach as I like to think all branch directors should be. At times when things were quiet and the branch was relatively problem free, I would feel quite proud of myself. It is a difficult task keeping all the areas of the branch running parallel while at the same time keeping "the powers that be" at head office happy. Because there are over twenty two thousand volunteers nation-wide with over two hundred branches, guidelines and procedures have to be met to aid consistency to the caller, who may call us from anywhere.

I used to lie in the bath, at the end of some do or other, and smirk to myself thinking, if only they could see me now. All those who thought I was nuts when I was going through the breakdown. Those who were less than kind to me when I needed care, not condemnation. Then I would think about my parents and family and I am really glad to be me. My children have now reached the age where we can relate to one another as adults. I want them to know and understand why they saw their mother almost destroy herself and her marriage because she was afraid if they knew the truth about her past, they would not love her. Over the years we as a family have had our moments and may well have more difficult times ahead of us, who knows. Our trials and tribulations have given Ray and me times of sadness and joy over the years. I know we have both faced them with courage. Because of my childhood and its long term affect on my adult life, I have seen more than my fair share of tears. I present just one side of the sad tale of a troubled family saga. All the others would have their own perception of how they coped with a childhood, in my opinion, void of love. We all see the world from a different angle. The one saving grace in my story is the way that the man who made a vow to love and cherish me in sickness and in health, fulfilled those vows against all the odds. His patience and understanding has been, and still is, limitless. His belief in me through all he has suffered for love of me, words cannot express. Ray could never have known, as no partner standing at the altar knows, what he would go through to keep those promises, but I know if he did, he would still say, "I do". Together we have laughed and we have cried, we have agreed and we have disagreed. We have not had the perfect marriage, and we have both failed sometimes. But looking back over our years together, it's not been far off perfect. And the best thing is, it's getting better every day. If I think of my life as a book I couldn't honestly say whether it would be a comedy or a thriller; a drama, or a tragedy; a love story with a happy ending, or a cliff-hanger, leaving the reader on the edge of their seat, waiting to see what happens next. Well even I don't know the answer to that. But you can be sure of one thing, it won't be boring. Only God knows what's in store for me now, and at the moment that's between Him and me.